TOWARDS POLITICAL EMPOWERMENT

TOWARDS POLITICAL EMPOWERMENT

Political Socialization and Political Participation of Tribal Community in Kerala

Dr. Rajeevan. R.

KALPAZ

Towards Political Empowerment : Political Socialization and Political Participation of Tribal Community in Kerala

Rs.540

ISBN: 978-81-7835-840-6

Published in 2010 in India by
Kalpaz Publications
C-30, Satyawati Nagar,
Delhi-110052
E-mail: kalpaz@hotmail.com
Phone : 9212729499

Laser Type Setting by: Rudra Computer Graphics, Delhi
Printed at : Chawla Offset Printers, Delhi

To,

The Patriotic Tribes of Kerala who Fought against the British even at the risk of their own survival.

Contents

Foreword

A striking political phenomenon in India since independence, particularly during the past two-three decades has been the emergence of subaltern groups as a source of political power. Of them tribal groups are probably the most important, as tribal leaders have come to occupy positions of power in states as well as at the centre. In recent times new states have been formed of predominantly tribal population across the central belt. Hence social scientists are now paying attention to the study of tribal groups with focus on how they are socialized into the democratic political process. Although tribal population in Kerala comprises only 0.5 percent of the total tribal population of India, it is gaining political attention in the state as part of the egalitarian concern for the marginalized. In fact the tribal people have a right to be heard and a right to stand on their own. Hence they organize and experiment with their own political forums within the modern political structures. Social and political scientists are now undertaking the study of political, social and economic dimensions of tribal life with increased interest.

Dr. R. Rajeevan is a leading political scientist with deep commitment to study of political and social phenomena relating to the state. He has rightly taken up a project of research on the tribal community of Kerala, which is gaining much political significance today. He has focused on the role of political parties and leaders in the political socialization process and on the changing attitudes of the groups towards the mainstream parties.

The method applied in the study is largely empirical and analytical. Primary data have been collected partly by survey, questionnaire and interview of tribal men and political leaders. The findings make it clear that the political future of the tribal community lies in their liaison with the mainstream politics and political parties.

Dr. Rajeevan's work is a remarkable contribution to the field of tribal study.

Prof. (Dr.) N. Jose Chander
Formerly Director,
Institute of Distance Education,
University of Kerala
and
Dean,
Faculty of Social Sciences,
University of Kerala

Preface

The tribes and their issues are seriously gaining the attention of social science researchers all over the world today. In the past, they were the concern of anthropologists alone. Today, the tribes themselves have changed their social and political behaviour considerably. As the states increasingly endeavoured to promote tribal welfare, the socialization, political participation and empowerment of the aboriginals attained new dimensions. The case of Kerala, a small state in Southern India with 0.5 percent of the total Indian tribal population is no exception.

As in other parts of the world, in Kerala too, tribes were the original owners of the rich forest lands. They had a history of once being economically prosperous and politically powerful. Their autonomous governing system remained intact for centuries until it was shattered by the British in India. Their indigenous life style and culture suffered greatly under the tribal policies of the alien rulers. The land reforms introduced by the 'Red men' which permitted easy intrusion of outsiders into tribal land, still proves to be a bane to tribal upliftment. The insensitive and biased administrative machinery of Kerala too, took sides with the politically strong infiltrations, adding their share to the disempowerment of these weaker sections of the society.

The two political coalitions which monopolized the political power of the state paid little attention to get the tribal protection laws implemented effectively in the state, though the tribal sections form active support structures to most of the political parties. The situation forced the tribals to evolve their own political organizations and methods of protest. The present study attempts to unveil the processes through which the tribes of Kerala attained political awareness and strength to stand up against those who disempowered them by taking away their rights to their natural habitat and livelihood.

I have been able to undertake this study thanks to a research grant awarded to me by the University Grants Commission. I am indebted to UGC to provide financial support without which this work would not have been materialized. My deep gratitude and indebtedness are due to the authorities of N.S.S College, Nilamel for their constant cooperation and help. I express my sincere thanks to the Kerala State Election Commission, Kerala State Planning Board, Department of Tribal Development, Forest Department and the officials of Vithura, Peringamala, Kulathupuzha, Themmala, Agali, Padur, Panamaram and Mananthavadi Grama Panchayats for their generous help and cooperation in gathering the data. My indebtedness are due to the respondents who cooperated with my survey. I am also thankful to KIRTADS, Kozhikode and KILA, Trissur for the information provided to me. I must also acknowledge the indispensable aid and encouragement of my family and friends. My thanks are due to Kalpaz Publications, Delhi for their efforts to bring out the work in its present form.

Rajeevan R.

1

Political Socialization and Political Participation of Tribal Community in Kerala: A Theoretical Perspective

Introduction

Of the three hundred million tribal people in the world, more than eight crores are in India. According to the 2001 census, the total tribal population of India is 83,580,634. They constitute eight percent of the total population of the country. Among them about 80 percent live in the 'central belt' extending from Gujarat and Rajasthan in the west, and across the states of Maharastra, Madhya Pradesh, Chattisgarh, Bihar, Jharkhand and Orissa, to West Bengal and Thripura in the east. Most of the remaining 20 percent live in the North Eastern states of Meghalaya, Mizoram, Nagaland, Arunachal Pradesh and Sikkim and in the union territories of Dadra & Nagar Haveli, Andaman &

Nicobar and Lakshadweep. A small number of them live in the South Indian states of Kerala, Tamil Nadu, Karnataka and Andhra Pradesh. Andhra Pradesh has the largest tribal population among the Southern states of India. 0.5 percent of the Indian tribal population live in Kerala.

There are 36 communities notified in the list of Scheduled Tribes in Kerala[1] (see table 1 in the appendices). As per 2001 census their population is 364189, which is 1.14 percent of the total population of the state[2] (see table 2 in the appendices). They are mainly concentrated in Wayanad, Idukki, Palakkad and Kasargod districts. 37.36 percent of the total tribal population of the state lives in Wayanad, which forms 17.43 percent of the total population of the district. Alappuzha district has the lowest concentration of tribal people[3] i.e., 0.86 percent. The 'Paniyan' tribe constitute the largest group with 67948 persons and the Konda Kapus tribe is the smallest group with only five members. It is estimated that there are more than 80,000 tribal families in Kerala. They live in about 4000 settlements. 23 percent among them reside in forests. Most of them speak local variants of Malayalam. But at the same time the tribals who belong to Palakkad and Idukki speak the mixed languages of Tamil and Malayalam and of Kasargod a mixture of Kannada and Malayalam languages.[4]

In the past, the tribals in Kerala, like other parts of the world, were the owners of forests and hills. They were economically prosperous and politically powerful. But the influence and pressures from the rulers of the main land disturbed their life, plundered their wealth and spoiled their power and influence. At last they lost their land and right in the forests. Land alienation is the pivotal issue of the tribals in Kerala at present. Landlessness among the tribes varies from 52 percent in Kurumans to 57 percent among the Paniyans and 61 percent among the Adiyans in Wayanad (see table 3 in appendices). In the northern districts of Kerala only 5 percent of the tribals live on agriculture. More than 80 percent work as agricultural labourers and only 0.5 percent are in government or semi government jobs. In the southern districts around 30 percent are engaged in agriculture, 40 percent are agricultural labourers and around 0.5 percent are engaged in white collar jobs.

The sex ratio of the tribals in Kerala is 996, where as for the general population it is 1,036.[5] As far as the education status is concerned, the pass percentage of tribal students in SSLC is 1.3 percent. Work participation among the tribes is higher than in the general category, at 46 percent compared with 31 percent for the general population. As per IRDP Survey, 40 percent of the tribes in Kerala are below the poverty line, compared with 25.75 percent for the general population. Wayanad district, which has the largest tribal population, also has the highest level of poverty at 60.38 percent. It is in this district that the largest number of poverty deaths have occurred among tribals. (Table 4 which shows the Deprivation Status of STs in basic amenities).

With the immigration of the mainland people to the tribal areas, the tribals were converted to agricultural labourers. Today the major tribal communities of the state like Paniyans, Adiyans,

Eravallan etc come under this category and even today majority of them are landless. But communities like Kurichchans, Kurumans, Malai Arayans, etc. to were traditionally settled cultivators and are relatively better than the agricultural labourer communities in terms of developmental indicators. However, forest regulations and alienation of land have made even those communities who were settled cultivators or shifting cultivators, agricultural labourers.[6] (see table 3, which shows Landless Tribal Families in Kerala – District wise).

During the period of India's freedom struggle itself, Mahatma Gandhi stressed the need for the emancipation and empowerment of these indigenous sections. After independence, Jawaharlal Nehru, the architect of modern India reiterated that the development in tribal areas should be slow and steady; the bureaucrats or the development personnel should be pro-tribal in mind and spirit and create an environment suitable to improve their process of socialization and the participation of the tribals in the development process. The issues of socialization, participation and empowerment of tribals were discussed in various forums.

The very essence of the concept of empowerment of the indigenous people was strengthened by the world summit for social development held at Copenhagen in March 1995. This summit proposed that empowerment was inextricably linked with increase in people's capacity to better utilize resources and opportunities. In the early years of the planning, India witnessed two significant changes in the economic and social realms:

introduction of the policy for economic reform and an intensification of the struggle of oppressed groups like the tribes for their rights to wealth and power. This is a new situation which Mohanty[7] describes as a shift from the old concept of 'growth with social justice' to 'development with empowerment.'

The Ninth five year plan 1997-2002 focused on the issue of the empowerment of tribals – that is, social and economic empowerment as well as social justice. The objective was to enable the tribes to exercise their rights freely, to enjoy the privileges and to lead a life of self confidence and dignity at par with other citizens of the country.

Even after five and a half decade since the promulgation of Indian Constitution and various steps adopted by the government for the development of the tribal communities, the condition of tribals in Kerala is one of exploitation, alienation of land and property rights, disempowerment and exclusion. The tribals have been the worst affected in the process that pushed them into the corner, advancing various dominant group interests. The existing paradigms of development resulted in seriously disturbing the tribal rights over their common property resources. This was possible because tribals across the state of Kerala were, and are the least powerful interest group.

With the close of the 20th century, the tribal sections of Kerala realized the loss that occurred to their community and the need to regain their power and rights. As a result the tribals began to question the developmental strategies adopted by the mainstream political parties. It should be noted that the tribals of Kerala are to a certain extent alienated from the mainstream political parties and are increasingly asserting their identity and culture. Out side these mainstream political parties, they formed their own organizations and even political parties for the protection of their rights and the promotion of their interests. Such a development shows that the political socialization process is taking place among the tribals of Kerala in a better way. It made them conscious of their conditions and they realized the need and necessity of political participation for their total empowerment.

At the same time we cannot close our eyes towards the initiatives made by the government and mainstream political parties of Kerala towards the development of the tribals. The state has already launched massive schemes for uplifting the tribal people and bringing them to the mainstream of the society. In the name of tribal development the state has spent a huge amount during the past years. But it is found that the laws and programmes have not achieved the target because of the influence of the vested interests like non tribal land owners and officials, who are exploiting them.

The process of political socialization and political participation among tribals strengthened in various forms for the purpose of empowering these sections. The government, the non governmental organizations, the political parties in Kerala, their own organizations and the officialdom have rendered good efforts for the cause of the tribals. The new Panchayati Raj Act accelerated the process of political participation and empowerment of the tribals in Kerala. Of the total 17,086 panchayat members of all the three tiers in the state, 193 persons are tribals. In the State Legislative Assembly, the tribals hold one seat. But in the Lok sabha and Rajya sabha, they have no representation from the state.

The tribal welfare programmes have also an important role in the process of political socialization and political participation. Their interaction with governmental and ITDP officials gave them more knowledge about politics and the need for participating in it. The political orientation from all these agencies and political recruitments helped them to achieve considerable degree of political culture. They acquired values, norms and attitudes towards political system through the process of political socialization and political participation.

Political Socialisation

The term political socialization refers to political learning i.e., a process of learning about politics. In the recent years, as a result of the impact of behavioural revolution in political science, there has been an attempt to make systematic study of this process by political sociologists. Since political socialization is a part of the general process of socialization any study of it requires a clear understanding of the concept of socialization.

The survival and continuity of a society depends upon the process of socialization, which means the process of acquiring social learning. Socialization is the master process whereby the individual comes to be at home in his own society. It is a moulding, inducing and absorptive social process interacting individuals and groups. Socialization is a mechanism whereby the relative endurance of the culture is maintained despite the essentially temporary membership of any given set of individuals.[8] Thus it is a means whereby the individuals acquire an understanding of values, norms and symbols of the society as well as knowledge, skill and disposition that enable them to participate as effective members of groups and society. From the point of view of the individual, socialization refers to what, when and how he learns and the personal consequences of this process on him.

To view socialization simply as the wide spread inculcation of traditional norms, values and attitudes or the shaping of a vast number of people so that they fit into and perpetuate a given social order, is clearly inadequate. Socialization indicates that part of learning which enables one to function more or less as an effective member of society. Socialization is the adaptation of the individual into the social culture i.e., the norms, values, beliefs, attitudes and needs of the society. It is a process of acquisition of attitudes, accumulation of behaviour and above all assimilation of traits and ideas. It promotes psycho-social, cognitive and moral development in man. Socialization is basically a learning process.[9]

Political socialization concerns itself with the orientation of individuals towards political objects and could be studied with reference to the elite, the mass, the deviant groups and social movements. If their attitudes, orientations and values change in the course of time, they get changed in their political culture also. Through this process, people are trained to have faith and conviction in political values. Political socialization is therefore the process of induction into political culture.[10]

The end product of political socialization is imbibing a set of attitudes, cognitions, values, standards and feeling towards the political system; its various rules and role incumbents. It also includes knowledge of values affecting feeling towards the inputs of demands and claims into the system and its authoritative outputs.[11] It is through this process that individuals became acquainted with the political system and inducted citizenship roles, acquire political orientation and patterns of behaviour and form orientations to political object. It is through this process that individuals come to terms with the political culture of a country. It determines his relation to political phenomenon.[12] Since the individual is continually being influenced in the shaping of his political attitudes, orientation and values, the process of political socialization goes on throughout his life. Like an individual, in this form the masses are also being socialized. In this respect, political socialization means socialization of masses, the process by which ordinary people develop their attitude towards their political system. From a political point of view, political socialization is extremely important, as the process by which individuals became involved to varying degrees in the political system in political participation.[13]

Political Participation

Democracy for its success as a form of government, needs active participation of members of the system. It means that the success of democratic process depends on the active participation of its members in the planning and the implementation of decisions. Political participation refers to a voluntary act of the individual in involving himself with the socio-political activities of his political system. Political participation varies according to the form of political system. It is the highest in the liberal democratic countries.

Through political participation members of a society play their role in the selection of rulers and in the formation of public policy. Through this process a close relationship is established between authorities and the people. To ensure people's participation democratic institutions must encourage people's active participation starting from the lowest practicable level. To increase the participation of the common people in the democratic governance, India, the largest democracy on the world, adopted a Panchayati Raj system.

The approach to tribal issues has experienced a shift from protection, welfare and development to participation and empowerment in the last decade of the twentieth century. This was possible due to the enactment of the Panchayati Raj Nagara Palika Act of 1992 through the 73nd and 74th Constitution amendments. It contains special provisions for increased participation of scheduled tribes through reservation of seats in the three tiers of Panchayati Raj institutions.

Review of Research and Development

Social Science research through out the world gave emphasis to the study of tribes. As far as our state is concerned, our colonial masters and their scholars, especially the missionaries conducted a number of anthropological research on tribals, which constituted a significant part of the literature of tribes. Most of the studies were limited to the study of the indigenous features of tribes - especially their culture. They emphasized the point that tribal people were kept away from the mainstream society. Some European anthropologists even went to the extent of describing their culture as 'eternal present' giving the impression that they are non-changing.

But after independence a number of Indian scholars got involved in the study of tribal issues. Modern methods and approaches of Social Science research were applied. Inter disciplinary approach with emphasis on psychology opened scope for Social Science research in a quite different manner. These researches show the realities in tribal life and their intensions to change the primitive attitudes. These researches could uncover a lot of truths and facts relating to their miserable life. These helped a lot to bring out effectively the issues of the tribal world and contributed much to change the situation of these marginalized sections.

In Kerala too tribal issues were seriously studied by scholars. A.A.D. Luiz's *Tribals of Kerala* (1962), P.R.A. Mathur's *Tribal Situation in Kerala*, Jacob John Kattakkayam's *Social Structure and Change among the Tribals* (1983), M. Kunhaman's *Development of Tribal Economy* (1989), G.B. Pillai's *Tribes of Attappady : A Socio-Economic Profile* (1989) are some among them. Further, a lot of studies have been made by various government, non-government agencies and academicians evaluating the tribal welfare programmes, their socio-economic status and the like, but their main concern have been the material development of tribals, changes in their socio-economic life, education, culture and the like. However, with the close of the twentieth century some studies were made on the political condition of the tribals in Kerala. Jos Chathukulam, C.V. Balamurali and K.N. Jayan's *Study on Special Component Plan and Tribal Subplan under Decentralized Planning Process in Kerala* (2000), Janu C.K. and M. Geethanandan's *Adivasi Grama Panchayathum Swayam Bharanavum* (Mal.) (2001), Janu C.K. and M. Geethanandan's *Muthangayilekkulla Thirichupokku Oru Sathyavangmoolam* (Mal.) (2003), P. Panur's *Keralathile Africa* (Mal.), *Ente Hrudayathile Adivasi* (2005) (Mal.), P.K. Prakash's *Anyadheen appedunna Bhoomi – Adivasi Bhoomi Prasnattinte Charitravum Rastriyavum* (Mal.) (2002), Dileep Raj's *Thantedangal* (Mal.) (2003) etc. are some among them. Even though these studies at times deal with tribal politics to a certain extent, none of them have made a serious attempt to thoroughly investigate the problem of political socialization, political recruitment and political participation of the tribal communities of Kerala state.

Hypothesis

1. The tribals in Kerala have achieved a good level of political socialization.

2. Political participation of tribals in Kerala strengthened especially after the passing of 73rd and 74th Constitutional amendments.

3. In accelerating the process of political socialization and political participation of tribals, the political parties in Kerala have a big role.

4. Government policies and legislations also have improved those processes.

Objectives

1. The chief objective of the study is to explore the role of the improved political socialization and political participation in the acceleration of the development of tribal community in Kerala.

2. To evaluate the performance of political parties and the leaders in socializing and recruiting the tribals.

3. To understand the major issues and challenges which hinder the political participation and empowerment of the tribals in Kerala.

4. To analyse the changing attitude of the tribals in Kerala towards the mainstream political parties and the scope of emerging their own social and political movements.

Inter-disciplinary Relevance

The study has definitely interdisciplinary relevance. Besides broadly pertaining to the field of political science and sociology, the study is equally relevant to psychology, economics and public administration.

Approach and Methodology

The methodology applied in the study is historical, analytical and empirical. Primary and secondary published data related to tribal areas has been extensively used for the purpose of developing the conceptual, theoretical and methodological framework of the study. An empirical analysis was made through field study, case study, and sample survey.

Primary data was collected through conducting a survey by visiting the tribal settlements in the selected Panchayats of the four districts Waynad, Palakkadu, Kollam and Thiruvananthapuram. The selection of the districts were made on geographical basis. The panchayats were selected on the method of simple random sampling. Given the peculiar historical background and ethnic composition of the tribal settlements, unstructured interviews were also conducted for qualitative data collection, especially to elicit informations on socio political transformations. Two types of questionnaires were framed for interviewing the common tribal people and the political leaders and representatives of the tribal community. Although it focused on the people belonging to tribal community, the researcher has also collected data from the officials and non tribals for gaining a more comprehensive picture of the political condition of tribals in Kerala.

Chapterization

The introductory chapter entitled "Political Socialization and Political Participation of Tribal Community in Kerala : A Theoretical Perspective" provides an overall description of the tribals in India, especially that of Kerala. It gives a theoretical frame to the concepts of political socialization and political participation. The chapter also discusses the research problem, review of research and development in the subject, interdisciplinary relevance, hypothesis, objectives and methodology of the study.

The second chapter, entitled "A Socio-Political Analysis of the Tribes in Kerala" portrays the various communities of tribals in the state emphazising their social, economic, educational and political status. It briefly analyses each tribal community individually.

The third chapter "Political Situation of Tribals in Kerala : A Historical Perspective" analyses the rich political heritage of the tribals in Kerala, the deterioration of their political power, the resistance movements of the tribals against colonialism, role of British colonialism in the disempowerment of tribals in Kerala and free India's approach to tribal issues.

The fourth chapter, "Tribal Land Alienation : Political Empowerment Becomes a Compelling Necessity" shows the picture of tribals, who were alienated from their land in various ways. This chapter also unravels how political parties and various governments of Kerala handled the issue. The chapter also throws light on the tribal movements that strive for their empowerment.

The fifth chapter "AGMS & RMS : New Experiments Towards Political Empowerment of Tribals in Kerala" provides a description on the formation and functioning of these two tribal organizations of Kerala. It also examines the factors behind the transformation of the tribal movement into a political movement, and also the service rendered by them in the political socialization, recruitment, participation and empowerment of the tribal sections in Kerala.

The sixth chapter "The New Panchayati Raj System: A Shift Towards Improved Participation and Empowerment of Tribal Community in Kerala" examines the New Panchayati Raj system in general and also its role in improving the political participation and empowerment of the tribal sections of Kerala. It also deals with the issues related to the transfer of responsibility to the tribals of Kerala through formal self government institutions – its achievements, short comings, major problems, alternative suggestions etc.

The seventh chapter is a face to face experience of the political socialization, participation and empowerment of the tribal community in Kerala. It provides the analysis of field survey report on the socialization and political participation of the tribal community of Kerala especially after the inauguration of the New Panchayati Raj system.

The eighth chapter i.e., the conclusion gives an account of the achievement of the project, summary of the findings and its social contribution.

Notes and References

1. According to the amendment of Scheduled Tribes list made by the Central Government in 2002, there are 36 Scheduled Tribe sects in Kerala. The Marati sect has been eliminated and the Scheduled Castes – Mavilan and Karimbalan have been included in the amended list. Accordingly there was an increase of 30,000 in the tribal population of Kerala.

2. Government of Kerala, *Scheduled Tribes Development Programmes* 2006-2007, Thiruvananthapuram, Department of Tribal Development, GOK, p. 1.

3. Government of Kerala, *Scheduled Tribes of Kerala at a Glance*, 2003, Kozhikode, KIRTADS, GOK, p. 10.

4. Ibid.

5. Ibid. p. 5.

6. Ibid. p. 10.

7. Mohanty. M., 2001, "On the Concept of Empowerment" in Debal K. Singha Roy (ed.) *Social Development and Empowerment of Marginalized Groups : Perspectives and Strategies*, New Delhi, Sage Publications, p. 23.

8. Robert Dowse and John Hughes, 1972. *Political Socialization*, London, Princeton University Press, p. 179.

9. Madhu Smitha Mishra, 2003, *Press and Political Socialization*, Delhi, Dominant Publishers and Distributors, p. 52.

10. Amal Kumar Mukhopadhyay, 1980, *Political Sociology : An Introductory Analysis*, New Delhi, Bhageheas and Co., p. 100.

11. Gabriel A. Almond, "Introduction : A Functional Approach to Comparative Politics" in Gabriel A. Almand and James S. Coleman (eds) 1960; *Politics of Developing Areas,* New Jersey, Princeton University Press, pp. 27-28.

12. Micheal Rush and Philip Athaff, 1971, *An Introduction to Political Sociology*, London, Nelson, pp. 13-14.

13. J.C. Johari, 1992, *Comparative Politics*, New Delhi, Sterling Publishers Pvt. Ltd., p. 138.

2

A Socio-Political Analysis of the Tribes in Kerala

A Brief Community wise study

Though the tribals constitute a small share of the total population of the state of Kerala, they are segregated as different communities in various districts. The census reports and various official studies differ in fixing the number of tribal communities in the state. There are 35 communities notified in the list of scheduled tribes in Kerala, as per 1991 census, which constitute 1.10 percent of the total population of the state. As amended by the Scheduled Castes and Scheduled Tribes Orders (Amendment) Act 2002 notified in the Gazette of India dated 08-01-2003, there are 36 tribal societies. At the same time a study made by PRG Mathur,[1] a specialist in the field gives the number of tribal communities in Kerala as 48 where as another scholar in tribal studies, K. Velappan[2] fixes the number as 53. The S.T population of the state is mainly concentrated in Wayanad, Idukki, Palakkad and Kasargode districts. A community wise analysis of the sociopolitical conditions of the scheduled tribes in the state are detailed in the chapter.

Adiyan

Adiyans are found in Wayanad district especially in the Taluk of Mananthavadi at Tirunelli, Trissileri, Kattikkulam, Panamaram and Bavali. This community has a total population of around 10,000. Traditionally followed a life of slavery, the landless Adiyans today are mostly agricultural labourers. Their dialect is a mixture of Malayalam and Kannada languages. Among them, 40 percent are literate. Even at present majority of them are landless, though a few are cultivators.

The hamlet of an Adiyan is locally known as 'Kudi'. The village where Adiyans live as a group is known as 'Kunt', with a headman called 'Kuntukaran'. At times there may be more than one 'kunt' in a village and they have a common chief known as 'Desakkaran', who is superior to 'kuntukaran'. Earlier each 'kunt' was under a landlord whose bounded labourers were the Adiyans.

The welfare schemes of the government has not brought about much changes in their living conditions. The attempts to empower them politically and socially by bringing them to the mainstream did not bear much fruit. They are also reluctant to modern education which stands in the way of their progress. The socialization process also is comparatively poor. They have also less interest in mainstream politics. So they hold limited positions as office holders in political parties or political institutions like PRIs.

Arandan

Traditionally nomadic hunters and gatherers, Arandans, locally identified as Aranadan or Eranadan, is found in the district of Malappuram. It is one of the smallest tribal community in the state with a population of around 200. Since they occupy a position at the bottom of the caste hierarchy, they are victims of severe caste oppressions. Their main occupation at present is non timber forest produce collection. They have a literacy rate of 40 percent.

Unlike other tribal sections, they have no strong group life. They do not show interest in cooperating with the mainlanders and are reluctant towards modern education. They have also no interest in mainstream politics and remain backward in the socialization process.

Eravallan

Eravallans are found in Palakkad district. Traditionally they were agricultural labourers attached to local landlords. They are generally a Tamil speaking community and their literacy rate is low i.e., 30 percent. They constitute only one percent of the tribal population of the state. They also have no strong group life. They are also reluctant towards modern education and modernization process. The attempts to empower them politically and socially by bringing them to the mainstream did not bear much fruit. They have less interest in mainstream politics and do not hold any notable post either in party office or in political institutions.

Hill Pulaya

They live mostly in the north eastern part of Idukki district and had migrated from Madhurai during the period of Pandya kings. There are two segments with in the community. One is the Karavazhi Pulayans who are agricultural labourers. The other is the Kurumba pulayans who make a livelihood by collecting forest produces. A section of this tribe had been converted to Christianity and they are economically well off. This Tamil speaking tribe constitutes about one percent of the total tribal population of the state.

The tribal settlement of hill pulayas is known as 'kudi' and 'Muppan' is the head of each 'kudi'. The 'Muppan' has an assistant called 'Thandukkaran' who carries out the orders of the 'Muppan'. Muppan, in the bygone days had a decisive role in controlling the lives of the tribals in his settlement. 'Pothusabha', the gathering of the entire tribal community in the settlement headed by Moopan would solve and take suitable decisions on various problems that arise in the settlement. Now the roles of the Moopan and pothusabha have become minimal. Their literacy rate is comparatively higher.

They show interest in receiving modern education and some of them have been well educated and employed. Some of them are showing interest in mainstream politics and posses political posts and positions. Their political socialization process is also comparatively good.

Irular, Irulan

One of the major ST communities in Kerala, Irulas stand sixth in population. They constitute about 7% of the total ST population in the state. They reside mostly in the district of Palakkadu in Attappady Hills. Outside the forest area, they live together in about 100 settlements. Irulars, traditionally, are settled cultivators but due to land alienation, today they have become either marginalized farmers or agricultural labourers. They undertake various agricultural activities after performing appropriate rituals.

The place where Irulars live together is called an 'Uru'. It's administration is undertaken by the local body called 'uru panchayat', with 'Moopan' as its head. Moopan play the role of a king or a judge in the 'uru'. His decisions remain unquestioned. Now a days though political parties could exert their influence upon the 'uru', to some extent Moopan's position remains more or less unchallenged.

There are seven sub castes among the Irular community. They are Vella, Devanan, Karunakan, Uppili, Karittiyan, Perithara, and Samban. Irulars have Tamil as their mother tongue. Their literacy rate is quite low.

The welfare schemes of the government brought about much changes in their living conditions. They are also showing interest towards modern education and mainstream politics. Their socialization process is also comparatively good.

Kadar

Kadars inhabit in the Vazhachal, Chalakkudi, Nenmara and Parambikulam divisions of Trissur and

Palakkadu districts. They use both Malayalam and Tamil for communication. They were traditionally engaged in hunting and gathering forest produces. Till recently they led an isolated life confined with in the woods with hardly any interaction with mainstream society. They have been identified as a Primitive tribal group by the government. Today they make a livelihood by collecting non timber forest produces and undertaking forest related works. Since their lives centre around forest and its resources, even today they maintain their reverence towards the forest.

The settlement of Kadars is known as 'Kani'. Each Kani has a head known as 'Moopan'. Among them, 'Moopan' is a non-hereditary post.

The various developmental schemes and measures of the government has not been strictly implemented to the progress of this sections of tribals. They have also very limited interest to join mainstream development. They are reluctant to modern education and have little interest in mainstream politics. The socialization process is also comparatively poor among Kadars.

Kanikkaran

Kannikkaran is an ancient community of tribals who are found in the southern forest region of Kerala and Tamil Nadu, ie in the erstwhile Travancore region. In Kerala, they are found mostly in the district of Thiruvananthapuram and to a small extent in the district of Kollam. Kanikkaran tribe holds the position of being the largest tribal community to reside in the forest regions.

There are two subdivisions among Kanikkaran, those dwelling in forest and those in plains. They were settled farmers traditionally, but majority of them are agricultural labourers and also NTFP collectors. They speak both Malayalam and Tamil. They form 5.13% of the total tribal population of the state and have attained a comparatively high literacy rate.

They led a well developed social life. They set up a democratic system of governance even before the so called civilized mainlanders. Decisions on important matters are taken by a committee of elders under the leadership of 'Muttukani', the tribal head. The undertake their occupations like cultivation, hunting and fishing collectively. Their present condition is deplorable. The mainlanders take advantage of their weaknesses, especially their affinity for alcoholic drinks. They are mostly under debt.

Kanikkars are known for their ethnic medicines. They have even gained patent for one of their ethnic medicines, i.e. Aarogyapacha.

Those Kanikkarans who are living in plains show interest in modern education. Already a good number of them received good education and employment in government and private services. Since, a large share of them are leading a rural life or reside in forests, the governmental measures to empower them politically and socially by bringing them to the mainstream did not bring the desired result. But the schemes and measures of the government had succeeded in changing their approach to mainstream life. A number of them are interested in mainstream politics and their participation in political parties is noticeable. A lot of them are holding political posts and positions and became office holders in Panchayat Raj Institutions. Their political socialization process also goes on comparatively well.

Kammara

This community is not found in Kerala. This is a Telugu speaking community found in former Madras Presidency. However they have been enumerated in various censuses in Kerala, even after the formation of Kerala. This is probably due to the reason that census enumerators record the name of the community of the individuals as revealed to them and validity of which is not verified by the enumerators. As per the census of 1991 only 123 Kammara tribals were reported. The community has been omitted from the ST list by the Scheduled Castes & Tribes orders (Amendment) Act 2002.

Kattunayikan

One of the major ST communities, Kattunayikan mostly resides in the district of Wayanad. The Kattunayikan, Cholanaikans and Pathinaikans may be one and the same community. The tribals living in the interior forest are called the Cholakkar (Cholanaickans). They mainly inhabit the Karulai range of the reserve forest and Chungathara range of the vested forests of Nelambur valley. The Kattunayikans are also known as Nayikkan or Thenkurumman.

Their growth rate is lower than the general growth rate of ST people. Their literacy rate is also very low i.e., 30 percent. They speak both Kannada and Malayalam.

Traditionally they are hunters and gatherers but today they are agricultural labourers. They also collect NTFP. They are experts at collecting honey and mahouting.

Their settlement is called 'keri' with 'Aadimuthali' as its head. Having identified as a primitive tribal group, the government has conceived and implemented special programmes for their development. Governmental schemes helped them a lot in bringing out considerable change in their primitive way of life. But the government programmes to empower them politically and socially did not bear much fruit. They are reluctant to receive modern education and it stands in the way of their progress. The socialization process also is comparatively poor. They have also less interest in mainstream political parties.

Kochu Velan

Kochu Velan is the synonym of the ST community Ulladan existed as item No.34 of the scheduled tribe list of Kerala. Ulladans of Pathanamthitta District is locally known as Kochuvelan. Traditionally they were the collectors of non timber forest produces and canoe makers. They speak Malayalam language and 80 percent of them are literate. Now a days most of them are agricultural labourers and take interest to sent their children to schools. Their total number is only around 50 and now they are conscious of their rights.

Kondakapus

This community is not seen in Kerala. This Telugu speaking tribal community is seen in Andhra Pradesh. However they have been enumerated in the census report and notified in the scheduled Tribe list of Kerala.

According to the 1991 census there were five Kandakapus in Kerala. The community has been omitted from the ST list by the Scheduled Castes & Tribes orders (Amendment) Act 2002.

Kondareddis

This is also a Telugu speaking community and is not seen in Kerala. This tribal community is found in Andhra Pradesh. However they have been enumerated in the census report of 1991 and notified in the scheduled tribes list of the state of Kerala. The community has been omitted from the ST list by the Scheduled Castes & Tribes orders (Amendment) Act 2002.

Koraga

The Koragas of Kasargode form a decisive primitive group among the tribals of Kerala. They speak a corrupt form of Tulu language. They are segmented mainly into three endogamous sub divisions viz, Jathy Koragas, Kuntu Koragas and Chappu Koragas. They maintain that both Jathy and Kuntu Koragas wore clothes even in olden days and lived in plain villages whereas the Chappu Koragas resided in forests. The Jathy Koragas claim that they are superior to the other two subdivisions. The community shares most of its cultural traits with the Koragas of South Canara District of Karnataka, where their major stock inhabit. They form around 0.60 percent of the total tribal population of the state and have a literacy rate of 50 percent. Their main economic activity is basketry. A considerable section of them work as agricultural labourers.

Now a days they send their children to modern education and they are vigilant enough to avail themselves of the benefits from government. Now most of them have pucca tiled houses constructed in colonies with the help of grants given by the government. Their hut is locally known as 'koppu'. They have their traditional tribal council which is presided over by the tribal headman called 'Gurikara'. He is assisted by his eldest nephew. The office of the Gurikara is hereditary and passes on from uncle to the eldest nephew. Crime and quarrels, cases of divorce, elopement, adultery etc were settled by the council after due deliberations. The council has almost ceased to function on account of their contact with modern democratic governments of the state. Traditionally they are matrilineal but not matriarchal. They have interest in mainstream political parties and their socialization process is also comparatively going on well.

Kota

Kota is a Tamil speaking ST community living in Wayanad district. This community is popularly found in the state of Tamil Nadu. According to the 1991 census, only 36 people of the community were reported. The community has been omitted from the ST list by the Scheduled Castes & Tribes orders (Amendment) Act 2002.

Kudiya, Melakudi

This community is found is Kasargod. Traditionally they were marginal farmers and even today their major economic activity is farming. They speak both Kannada and Malayalam. Their literacy rate is more than 60 percent. Majority of their families hold land and their number is around 1000. Today, they follow the life style of the people of the mainland.

They are sending their children to schools and try to avail themselves of the schemes of the government for their development. They could change their living conditions to a certain extent. They also welcome modern education. Their socialization process also is comparatively good. They show interest in mainstream political parties.

Kurichan

One of the major ST communities in Kerala, Kurichans are found in the districts of Wayanad, Kannur and Kozhikodu. They were settled cultivators traditionally and had sufficient land holding. Currently they are mostly marginal farmers. They speak a dialect of Malayalam language. Kurichian stands ahead of other tribal groups in education and economic development. They consider themselves superior to other tribal groups and even observe the practice of untouchability.

The ancestors of Kurichan were the warriors of Pazhassi Raja. They were believed to be send by the Raja of Travancore at the request of Pazhassi Raja to defend the attack of Tipu Sultan. They are well versed in guerilla warfare and archery.

They owned large acres of farm land and did all agricultural activities by themselves. They were also good hunters. The place where Kurichar live in groups is called 'Mintam'. They follow joint family system. The head of the family is 'pittan' and the agricultural lands and products will be under his custody. He had great hold over the other family members but now his hold has begun to shake.

Their traditional well being along with the modern developmental schemes and measures to promote the STs, upgraded the Kurichars to a comfortable living condition. Their approach to modern education is also positive, which provided a good educational and employment status to them. Their socialization process is also satisfactory. They also show interest in mainstream political parties. So they hold position as office bearers of political parties and hold office in all the three layers of Panchayat Raj Institutions.

Kurumans

Kurumans belong to Wayanad and lead their lives there as forest dwellers. Some of them occupy large acres of forest land. Traditionally they are cultivators and cultivate rice, ragi, plantain, coffee, pepper and ginger. They were good at archery too. They have attained progress in education and other sectors of life though not as much as Kurichars.

Politically they are ahead of other tribal sectors. They have even had an M.L.A, Radha Raghavan from among them, who effectively raised the issues of tribals in the Kerala Legislative Assembly.

The tribal settlement is known as Kudi also called 'Kudumbam'. 'Valiyamuthan' (Porunnavan), the eldest among them, heads the kudi. A number of 'kudis' in the area also had a common head called Karanavar, who has an authoritative role among the Kurumans.

Now a days Kurumans are in good relations with other tribal sections of Wyanad as well as the outsiders (mainlanders). They also welcome modern education.

So they have a large number of highly educated and government employed members. They also participate in mainstream politics and are office bearers in various political parties. They are also office bearers of Panchayat Raj Institutions at the three layers.

Maha Malasar

It is a wandering tribe residing in the hills of Nelliyampathy, Kollamkodu and Parambikulam of Palakkad district. As forest laws became rigid, they were forced to lead a settled life. They are hunters and gatherers. They speak Tamil. According to 1991 census, only 36 people were reported. Their literary rate is also very low.

Their settlement is known as 'Kudi' or 'Kani', headed by 'Moopan'. The post of Moopan is hereditary. He has an authoritative voice over the kudi even now. The welfare schemes of the government has not brought about much changes in their living conditions. The attempts to empower them did not bear much fruit. They are also reluctant to modern education and this stands in the way of their progress. They have also less interest in mainstream politics.

Kurumbas

The Kurumbas found in Attappady hills of Palakkad district is considered as a primitive tribal group. They are traditionally hunters, food gatherers, and shifting cultivators. Out of the 1820 Kurumbas (1991 census) 1558 are living in forests. Majority of them (1344) are living in 14 settlements of Attapady situated in the Mannarghat Taluk of Palakkad District. It has an area of 765 square kilometers and is mostly covered by dense forests. 214 of them are living in the Tirthamala settlement of Marayur range in the Munnar Division of Idukki District. They speak the language of Tamil and only thirty percent of them are literate.

The settlements in which they live is called 'Uru' and each Uru has a headman called 'Moppan'. He is assisted by two deputies, the 'Kurutalai' (peon) and the 'bandari' (cashier). 'Mannukkaran' (one who knows the soil) is another popular personality among the Kurumbas. Mannukkaran officiates, as priest, all the rituals associated with sowing and harvesting. The post of Mooppan is a hereditary one. He is powerful and various issues are settled under his supervision. Even today, the Mooppan is discharging his powers effectively. Definitely the Kurumbas have a well organized social life and their traditional tribal council is very efficient. The tribal council is known as 'Uru Panchayath.'

When an extraordinary situation arises either due to increase in the number of 'Kuras' (houses) or differences of opinion with the Mooppan, there gets created a new mooppan together with the formation of a new 'uru'. The new 'uru' also elects a new 'uru Panchayath' and a new Bandari. The wife of Mooppan, known as 'Mooppathi' and the wife of Bandari, 'Bhandarichi' are also respectable personalities.

Among the Kurumbas the problem of transfer and alienation of land has not arise at all because their habitat is entirely within the reserve forest.

The welfare schemes introduced by the government has brought about some changes in their living conditions. They have begun to receive modern education and embrace democratic way of life. They also cooperate with mainstream political parties. Their political socialization process is also advancing.

Malai Arayan

Traditionally settled cultivators, they are one of the major ST communities of the state. They reside in the districts of Idukki and Kottayam. With almost 85% of literary rate, they are foremost among the tribal communities of Kerala to acquire education and enter into government services. They were settled cultivators in the past but now they are marginal farmers. They themselves claim that they are the ancestors of Maharshi Veda Vyasa. They also claim that they are aristocratic and call themselves as Giri Brahmins (Hill Brahmins). They speak Malayalam. They constitute about 8 percent of the total tribal population of the state.

The welfare schemes introduced by the government helped them a lot to change their living conditions. The attempts to empower them politically and socially by bringing them to the mainstream also succeeded partially. They have begun to send their children to modern educational centres. They are also participating in mainstream political activities and social movements. They are conscious of the need and necessity of unifying the tribals for the protection of their rights and strongly advocate the reinstating of the alienated lands of tribals.

Malai Pandaram

This community is also a very small tribal sect in Kerala which constitute about one percent of the total tribal population of the state. They believe themselves to be migrants from the Tirunelveli forests of Tamilnadu to Kerala forests. One third of them are living in the forest settlements of Thenmala, Punalur, Konni and Ranni forest divisions of Kollam and Pathanamthitta districts. They were traditionally collectors of forest produces. They are landless and their major economic activity is the collection of Non Timber Forest Produces. Their language is a mixture of Tamil and Malayalam. About 50 percent of them are literate.

They receive various types of assistance from government which brought about much change in their living conditions. Generally they are reluctant to modern education. At the same time they cooperate with the mainstream political parties.

Malai Vedan

Malai vedan resides in the districts of Kollam and Pathanmthitta with a literacy rate of 62 percentage. The studies made by KIRTADS has identified that the scheduled caste, Vedan community living in the plains are ethnographically the same community. They claim themselves to be the predecessors of Maharshi Valmiki. There are four distinct Illams (groups) with in the community. They are Venadan, Kunnadan, Mayilar, and Koviriyan. The community is landless and their major economic activity is NTFP collection and agricultural labour. They constitute about two percent of the total tribal population of the state.

In each settlement, they have a Mooppan. In the past Mooppans enjoyed a lot of powers. But now he is only a ceremonial head. The welfare measures of the government have not brought about much change in their living conditions. They have very few opportunities to acquire modern education. Lack of opportunities together with the lack of proper awareness keeps them under educated. They have interest towards mainstream political parties and at the same time they admit the fact that they (political parties) are not providing anything substantial to them.

Malakkuravan

According to the studies made by KIRTADS, Malakkuravan community is not found in Kerala. However, in some parts of Pathanamthitta and Kollam districts, the scheduled caste Kuravans living in the hilly areas are claiming scheduled tribe Malakkuravan status. They are around 500 in number (as per the census of 1991) and they are agricultural labourers.

Malasar

This community is found in Nelliyampathy and Parambikulam forests of Palakkad district. Traditionally they were hunters and gatherers. Today their major economic activity is NTFP collection. They speak Tamil. They constitute only 0.33 percent of the total tribal population of Kerala. Their literacy rate is also very low ie., 30 percent.

Malasars dwell in permanent hamlets in the forests. Their colony is called 'pathi'. Each pathi has a headman called Mooppan. The man in the pathi second to Mooppan is Vandari. Mooppan's wife is 'periamma'. The post of Mooppan is not hereditary. He is elected by the members of the 'pathi' after taking into consideration his leadership qualities. He cannot repudiate the post by himself, but only after selecting another Mooppan by the members of the 'pathi'. Mooppan takes care of the various issues in the colony. Earlier Mooppan's words were the final one. But now his status is lowered. The community is reluctant to receive modern education. They also have no confidence in the mainstream political parties. But at the same time the young generation is taking part in the activities of political parties.

Malayan

The Malayan tribe makes a livelihood by collecting forest produces. So they are rightly called Malayan, which can be defined either as the man on the hills or the man who makes a livelihood by the hills. They merely live in the forest region from Thundathil to Parambikulam, mostly in the forest ranges of Thrissur and Ernakulam Districts. Though the population of Malayan Community is 7542 as per 1991 census, it might not be very accurate, as many of the non tribals are bogusly claiming Scheduled Tribe Malayan status in different parts of the state, particularly in Idukki District.

This Malayalam speaking community has two sub sections. They are Nattumalayans and Kongamalayans. Malayans remain backward in education. But a few received college education and government employment. Though many parents are willing to educate their children, their living conditions and other inconveniences stand in their way. The political socialization process is not going on well.

Mannan

Mannans are found in Idukki District. Out of the 7085 Mannans (1991 census) 4426 people (1021 families) are living in 16 forest settlements. Their language is a mixture of Malayalam and Tamil. It is assumed that Mannans migrated from Tamil Nadu. They were efficient in warfare and received Kingship and Kingdom from the Raja of Cochin.

Mannans have two spiritual leaders. They are known as Gurukkals. Below the Gurukkals, there are five Mannans (Kings) at the apex of the administration. One among them is elected as their head who comes to be called Rajamannan (Maharaja). The headquarters of the present Rajamannan is Kozhimala.

Below the Mannans (Kings) there are heads for each 'kudi' (Settlement). He is known as 'kanikkaran'. In the olden days they carried out an administrative system much better than their counterparts in the plains. Among the tribal sects in Kerala, Mannans still retain the traditional tribal governmental system though in name.

They are settled cultivators in the past. But now have been reduced to become marginal farmers. They are backward in education. The number of tribals to receive higher education and government employment is almost nil. They have also limited interest in main stream political parties.

Marati

Maratis are found in Kasargod district. They speak Kannada language. They constitute more than eight percent of the total tribal population of Kerala according to the census report of 1991. 60 percent of them are literate. Traditionally they were marginal farmers. They show interest in sending their children to schools. They are also aware of the various benefit schemes of the government and are availing themselves of the benefits. They co-operate with mainstream political parties and its activities. Some of them assume powerful positions in political parties and Panchayat Raj Institutions. But the community has been omitted from the ST list by the Scheduled Castes & Tribes Orders (Amendment) Act 2002.

Muthuvan, Mudugar, Muduvan

All these are synonymous of the same tribal group. Most of them dwell in the district of Idukki. They are also found in Palakkad, Malappuram and Kozhikkodu. In the forest, they are concentrated in the Munnar forest division and Chinnar Wild Life Sanctuary of Idukki district. Ten settlements are found in the Malayattur forest division, eight in Nilambur North Forest division and one in Parambikulam. They stand second in population among the forest dwelling tribe of Kerala. They constitute 5.5 percent of the total tribal population of Kerala. They speak Tamil. They are marginal farmers and also engage in NTFP collection.

The place where Muduvans live is called 'Kudi'. Their headman is called 'Mooppan' or 'Kanikkaran'. The post of Mooppan is hereditary. Mooppan still retains a powerful hold on his kudi. They made benefit out of governmental schemes especially for building houses. But they are far behind in getting educated. Till recently they didn't send their children, especially girls, to schools. The scope for higher education and government employment is almost nil. They have very limited interest in mainstream political parties. Political socialization process paces very slow among Muduvans.

Palleyan, Palliyan, Palliyar

This Tamil speaking tribe lives in the eastern regions of Idukki District. They have four settlements inside the forest in the Kumoly range. Majority of them are plantation labourers (tea plantation) and they were brought to Idukki by British from adjoining Madurai District (Tamil Nadu), particularly from Bodinayakanur Taluk for clearing the forests. They constitute 1.5 percent of the total tribal population of the state.

They lead a collective life in their settlement called 'kudi'. The headman was called 'Kanikkaran' and his post was hereditary. Now the post of the kanikkaran is replaced by the colony president. They stand united behind the president. The president is elected every three years. Party politics also plays its role in the election of their president. Educationally they are backward. But at the same time they have much interest in mainstream political parties.

Paniyan

Paniyan is the largest Scheduled Tribe of Kerala, ie., about 22 percent of the total tribal population of the state. Majority of them are living in the district of Wayanad. They are also found in Kozhikodu, Kannur and Malappuram. Below ten percent of them are living in forest settlements. Traditionally they were wandering people in the forests and they were forced to work in the land of land lords as bonded labourers. Paniyan is now among the few tribes of Kerala having no sub castes. They speak paniya language, a crude form of Malayalam language.

Being bonded labourers to landlords, the Paniyans resided near the farm lands of landlords in small groups. Such settlements known as 'Pera' has a headman, called 'Janmi.' He was the representative of the landlord and he had the responsibility to supervise the Paniyas in their labour. The Paniya Janmi was not only the leader of the Paniyas, but also was the connecting link between the Paniyas and the landlord. Thirty five percent of them are literate. But rarely, they are sending their children to higher education. The very few Paniyas who had entered the government service are doing lower grade jobs. Though they show interest to mainstream politics to some extent, few of them rise up to responsible positions in political parties and public office.

Ulladan

Ulladan is the synonym of the scheduled tribe community of Kochu Velan. They are residing in the districts of Pathanamthitta, Kottayam, Idukki, Thrissur, Ernakulam, Alappuzha and Kollam. The Ulladans of Pathanmthitta district is locally known as Kochuvelan. Traditionally they were the collectors of non timber forest produces and canoe makers. They speak Malayalam. They constitute about five percent of the total tribal population of the state.

Ulladans have adopted the life style of the main landers. Though they are economically and educationally backward, comparatively a good number of them have received higher education and entered into government service. Now a days they show interest in giving proper education to their children. Their settlement is called 'Kudi' with 'Kanikkaran' as its headman. Majority of them are agricultural labourers.

They have interest in mainstream political parties and some of them are in office in almost all political parties and in public institutions like Panchayat Raj Institutions.

Urali

The Malayalam speaking community is mainly concentrated in the districts of Idukki, Pathanamthitta, Kottayam and Wayanadu. Half of them are in Idukki and one fourth are in Wayanadu. Among them, half are dwelling in the settlements in forests. They have been converted to Christianity on a large scale especially in Mathaipara, Palukavu, Kurivankandam, Kanjiyar, Kozhimala, Ottitti and Vagaman. This community is landless and their major economic activity is NTFP collection. They claim themselves to be the royal tribe in the forest and they were good warriors. Their settlement is called 'kudi' and its head is Kanikkaran. They constitute 3.22 percent of the total tribal population of the state. Having a comparatively high rate of literacy, they are also interested in higher education. They have also interest in mainstream politics.

References

1. Mathur, P.R.G, 1977 *Tribal Situation in Kerala*, Trivandrum : Kerala Historical Society, p. 4.

2. Velappan. K, 1994 *Aadivasikalum Adivasi Bhasakalum*, Thiruvananthapuram : Kerala Bhasha Institute, p.22.

3

Political Situation of Tribals in Kerala: A Historical Perspective

Like other parts of the world, the tribals in Kerala were the owners of the forests and hills. They are believed to be the earliest settlers in the land. They are generally called the 'Adivasis' implying 'original inhabitants'. Since these areas were physically isolated and geographically segregated, for centuries they lived in isolation. This isolation helped them to preserve their customs, traditions, faith, belief etc. to a large extent. They were politically organized and economically powerful in their own way.

Each tribal sect was politically controlled by the traditional modes of leadership. Their life was totally controlled by their chiefs. The people enjoyed full liberty to use forest products. They cultivated various crops for their own consumption. Their diet not only contained the required calories but was balanced with ample milk, flesh, fruits etc. They were free from slavery and exploitation.

Mostly they led a carefree life; singing and dancing was an integral part of their communal life. At least once in a month (especially full moon days) in the middle of the hamlet, men and women gathered round a bonfire and sang and danced. The permission and presence of the tribal chief was a noted feature there. Their rituals and celebrations were conducted according to the directions of the tribal chief, who also was their chief priest. As elsewhere in the past, the tribal state too inextricably intermingled both politics and religion which formed its power of authority. When feudalism got strengthened, the tribal chiefs established good relations with the feudal lords and native kings. There is also evidence for gentleman's agreement between the native rulers and tribal chiefs. On several occasions, the native rulers extended their help to the tribals during times of poverty, starvation, disease, aggression from animals etc. But the native kings never tried to intrude into the geographical, political, cultural or economic arena of the tribals.

In their turn, the active kings sought the help of tribal chiefs during times of attacks and wars from outside. No native ruler tried to violate the forest limit and never made unnecessary interferences in tribal affairs. The political power and status of the tribals were respected. The relationship between the plains and the forest of the period proved to be a fine example of value based politics.

As kingdoms expanded and native kings became more and more powerful, the tribal chiefs also tried to become powerful. Even though there is no clear historical evidence for it, it is believed that a few tribal kingdoms grew up in Kerala and some of these tribal kings were very powerful. The Kurumars of Waynad believe that they belonged to the royal family of Vedas, who resided in the Velukkumbam fort near Pulpalli.[1] At that time, they were the rulers of the entire Wayanad region. The veda kings were very powerful and well known warriors. This was a permanent headache to the kshrtriya kings of neighbouring states like Kottayam, Kurumbanadu and Kumbala. These rulers tried to over power the tribal kingdom several times in various ways. Finally they resorted to treachery to defeat the tribal king. Subsequently, the northern Wayanad was annexed to the kingdom of Kottayam and southern Wyanad to Kurumbanad. After that Wyanad was divided into eleven villages under eleven Nair feudal lords. These Nair lords enslaved the Kurumars and made them their agricultural labourers.[2] Even under such circumstances they need not had to surrender their forest rights.

In those days private land rights was an alien concept of the tribal society who lived on simple modes of production. Each tribal hamlet was occupied by only one tribal sect. Land and resources in the hamlet were commonly owned. It was the tribal chief with the advise of the village committee who distributed the land among the people for cultivation. It is believed that the tribals had from the very beginning their own system of village government controlled by the tribal chief and assisted and advised by a tribal village committee. The main function of this government was the protection of the community from outside communities, maintaining law and order and settlement of disputes between families.

In the traditional political organization of the tribals in Attappadi, in Palakkad district the Mooppan was the apex. There were three important political positions: the Bandari, Kuruthalai and Mannokkaran, the former two to assist the Mooppan in administrative matters and ensure internal discipline and security of the groups, and the latter, to assist the matters related to agriculture. It was the Mannookkaran who first sowed the seeds, performed certain rites and rituals and gave offerings to Gods and selected the land for shifting cultivation. All political positions, except that of Mannookkaran were hereditary in nature, the law of descent being from father to son. The Mooppan presided over all the religious and cultural ceremonies and was the arbiter in case of disputes. He was also the connecting link between the government officials and the families in the tribal settlement. The autonomous governing system of the tribals remained intact for centuries until the arrival of the British invaders.

The political power and influence of the tribals in Kerala decelerated during colonial period. The British raj tried to weaken the tribal power in various forms. The tribals were one of the first to fight against the atrocities of the British rule. They fought against the British even at the risk of their own survival. This happened long before the fight against the aliens began in the plains.

As the defenders of their soil, the tribals proved their love and affection to their state in a number of times. In the struggle that Pazhassi Raja fought against the British, the powerful tribal sect in Wyanad the Kurichchias, with all their might fought against the British with bows and arrows. The Kurichchia war under their leader Thalakkal Chandu made serious set back to the British forces in defeating Pazhassi Raja.[3]

In its true sense, Kurichia revolt that took place in Northern Kerala was a revolt of the people. It gives a different dimension to the early phase of freedom struggle in Kerala. The British who suppressed the Pazhassi revolt tried to establish their supremacy in Wyanad there by making the tribal life troublesome. A lot of tribals were captured by the British officials, who made them their slaves.

The new Tax Reform introduced by the British was an attempt to destroy the tribals in Malabar. It generated a sense of discomfort among them. According to the New Tax Reform, those who used to pay tax in kind were to pay it in cash. Land surplus and labour shortage was the condition that prevailed during the period in North Malabar.[4] It was a tactics to make the tribals landless and force them to work as wage labourers.[5] It was a means to exploit tribal land and work force. If someone failed to pay the tax promptly, he was cruely punished. This created a general atmosphere of fear that the policies of the British will destruct the indigenous life style and culture of the tribals. The disgruntled Kurichchias joined hands with Kurumbars, another tribal sect there and under their leader Ramanambi started fight in March 1812.[6]

The revolt of the tribal sects showed their organized power and political will. Even though they had no modern weapons, the Kurichchiars and Kurumbars made careful preparations for their last fight against the British. There are evidences that they made arrows with the iron bars of bridges. The British sub-collector Thomas Harve Babar had recorded that the aim of these revolutionaries was to quit the 'flat headed' ones.

The revolt of the sons of the soil spread to the whole of Malabar. The tribal priests encouraged them proclaiming that they have the support of their gods. The revolutionaries gave their followers the advice that they must remain one in the name of the gods of Wayanad - 'Pulpalli Murikkans'. Even those Kurichchiars who were employed under the British, changed sides and joined the revolutionaries.

Malabar with all its major hill tracts came to be controlled by the revolutionaries. They attacked police stations and cruelly ill treated the Englishmen upon whom they came across. The British realized the power of the tribals and imported more military force from Mysore and Kanara and brutally suppressed the revolt. Even with the strong support of the local people, the tribals had to surrender before the British. On May 8, 1812, the revolt was completely suppressed.[7]

The revolt really resulted from the wrong policies of British towards tribal lands. The land policy and regulations implemented by the British through recordings and complicated measurement processes were totally alien to the tribals, who were not able to understand and assimilate the new system. As a result they did not bother to get ownership deed for their land.[8] They traditionally thought that they have a right to make access to the natural resources, which constitute their environment. They considered it to be their privilege to exercise control over the surrounding resources. The forest and forest produce constitute an important subsidiary means of their livelihood. Restriction on the use of forest, which is their land, is to curtail the basic rights of the tribals. The policies of the British raj mobilized the tribal people in revolt against the rulers. Even thought these were very relevant revolts, it rarely attracted the attention of the leaders involved in anti colonial struggle.

Apart from the British, the policies of the native kingdoms too influenced the tribal life of the state during the pre-independence period. Before the formation of the state of Kerala, different regimes existed in the Travancore-Cochin area and the British controlled Malabar region, which had differential impacts on each tribal group. Majority of the tribals in Kerala reside in the district of Wyanad, which was under British Malabar until 1947. The peculiar feature of Wyanad is the long stretches of paddy fields and plains. When there was the shortage of farm hands to work at these paddy fields, the aborigines especially the Paniyas and Adiyas, were brought there. When in the second phase of the 19th century plantations began to develop, these tribal people were made to work there as labourers. This was the beginning of their labourisation.[9]

In the princely state of Kochi, the tribals were less in number. They were mostly engaged in collecting forest products for commercial purposes. They came under the direct control of the Kochi government, when the government monopolized the forest area by the close of the 18th century. The government followed a protective and friendly approach towards them. In 1905 the Kochi Forest Act was passed. As a result most of them turned out to be agriculturists, rather than agricultural labourers.

In the princely state of Travancore, the state had maintained a protective policy towards the tribal people and their lands. Through various Acts and Proclamations, the Travancore government ensured the property right of all the tribal sections. For example, in 1903 a Hillman Settlement Act was promulgated to offer special protections to tribes.[10] The Hillman Rules published in old Travancore on December 14, 1891 also provided provisions for tribal protection.

Attapady, which is the second largest in tribal population has a different history. Till mid 1950s the area was unaccessible to other people. The original settlers at the place were hill tribal sects like Irular, Mudugar and Kurumbar. They had to leave their homeland to barren lands following the on rush of immigrants from the main land.

It is a truth that hills and forest were the main source of life and livelihood for the tribals. Land and forest rights are basic to their life. The condition of the tribals separated from their land and forest could be like that of a fish out of water.[11]

It was the British who for the first time adopted certain policies, which resulted in the alienation of tribals land and forest rights. The lands and forest, which the tribals enjoyed for ages was privatized by the British for plantations. Later the outsiders were allowed to come and settle in the tribal land with force and forcible consent.[12] Consequently, the adivasi population was uprooted and alienated from their land. This resulted not only in the lose of their livelihood but also in their cultural alienations. To conclude the tribals and indigenous people had became the first victims of conquest and colonization in the political history of Kerala. Even though India got independence and democratic and constitutional government was established, the same process of alienation and disempowerment had repeated in the case of tribals in Kerala. After ages of marginalisation and dispossession, many indigenous groups physically disappeared, which has been termed as ethnocide or cultural genocide, meaning disappearance of sub national ethnic units.

Free India's Approach to Tribal Issues

When India became a free nation, the leaders of India had clear vision on tribal issues. The first prime minister of India, Jawaharlal Nehru was famous for his pro tribal policies. His knowledge and vision on tribal issues was expressed in his famous statement that "tribal problems should be viewed in their own context, as the tribal economy cannot be separated from their cultural disposition and sovereignty." One may think that Nehru was speaking as a Prime Minister showing sympathy for poor tribal subjects, but infact he loved tribals as they were more disciplined and democratic than most other groups in India. They are more civilized in their own way.[13]

Being an exponent of Indian history, Nehru examined tribal issues from a broader historical perspective. He underlined that tribal history in India was a constructed, concocted and distorted history, and was not written on the basis of true evidence. The colonial ethos placed the tribe on a wrong footing in the history of Indian civilization. The British officers purposefully segregated the tribes from Indian society and projected them as different from mainstream civilization. Looking at such distortions by colonial historians, Nehru put forward two propositions. First that 'most historical writings have sought to reflect man's disunity and therefore much of what has been written about the tribes in various parts of India or elsewhere is information or conjecture, needing fresh examination and a new perspective', second that 'the creators of this history were foreign historians or anthropologists who intended to open up the mysteries of savage culture on Indian soil without understanding the social coherence between tribes and non-tribes'. Such a colonial ethos has undermined the whole concept of the study of tribal life and this is why we do not have coherent logical or broadly applicable definitions of a tribe.[14] He conceptualized the constitution led safeguards as the 'Panchsheel' policy, which emphasized that the tribals as a cultural group should not be disturbed in the name of developmental programmes.

The Constituent Assembly of India and its sub committee on tribal affairs had devised a structure of constitutional provisions for providing legal safeguards to millions of tribes living in different parts of the country. There are twenty articles in the Indian

Constitution that provide protection directly and indirectly to the tribals. Prominent among them were included in the sixth schedule of the Constitution to compel the concerned state governments to take specific care of them and allow them to lead an undisturbed cultural life. The Constitution aimed to uplift and bring the hither to backward sections of the Indian population including the tribals into the mainstream of the Indian life and society by bringing them under the country wide social, political and administrative network. Since it was declared as a national goal, the central as well as the state governments adopted strategies and policies for the development and empowerment of the tribal people.

From the First Five Year Plan itself the government of India has formulated a series of development policies for the welfare of tribals. Nehru, the first Prime Minister of India, who was also the father of Indian planning system, had strongly supported the idea that the tribes should be able to enjoy the advantages of modern science and technology, but certainly not at the cost of the rare and precious values of their life. He also insisted that the development process of tribal people should be slow and steady, the personnel involving in their development should be pro-tribal in mind and spirit, and should create the environment for increasing participation of tribals in the process of their development.

From the first five year plan to the tenth five year plan, a number of schemes were implemented under tribal development programmes. The diverse programmes have ranged from infrastructure building to empowerment, from collective welfare to family and beneficiary oriented development schemes and from solitary area development to integrated area development. The latest schemes focused on the issue of empowerment - that is social, economic and political empowerment as well as social justice. The objective was to enable the tribes to exercise their rights freely, to enjoy the privileges and to lead a life of self-confidence and dignity at par with other sections of the people.

The Kerala government's deep concern for the welfare of the tribal people manifests in the launching of several policy initiatives and the creation of a wide network of development administration to bring about a radical change in the life style of this people. About two percent of the total state plan outlay has been set apart for the development of scheduled tribes. Schemes for their uplift are formulated both at state level and Panchayat level. Funds are also allotted to various departments such as Kerala Electricity Board, Kerala Water Authority, Education, Health, Fisheries and Animal Husbandry for project based activities of tribal development. The educational projects include construction, renovation and management of nursery schools, pre and post matric schools, Model Residential Schools/Ashram Schools, Boys' and Girls' hostels and Vocational training institutes; tutorial schemes for school going students and failed students that provide special coachings to students of high school and Plus I & II classes to increase the percentage of pass; Financial assistance for excursion and Study Tour (Bharat Darshan) to ST students of Plus two, Degree, PG Degree,

Professional and Diploma courses who excel in their studies; Peripatetic Education to Primitive tribes, a scheme based on single teacher programme in which the teacher is expected to visit the identified tribal settlements and provide education so as not to uproot tribals from their isolated settlements; and the scheme guaranteeing quality education to students belonging to extremely poor tribal sections of Kerala.

There are schemes for conducting cultural programmes, anti-liquor propaganda, digital documentation of the life style, culture, and their day to day activities, entrance oriented coaching to ST students who seek admission for professional courses, assistance to ST students who study profession courses by providing study materials, dress and other items, honorarium to counselors engaged in the prematric hostels and Model Residential Schools, provision of additional apprenticeship to ITC/ITI passed ST candidates, annual state level festival of the students of MRS, and allotting incentives to ST youths talented in Arts and Sports.

The government also provide health care package to tribals suffering from various diseases. Organizing medical camps, providing transportation facilities to patients to nearby hospitals, providing nutritious food, providing drugs unavailable in hospitals and financially assisting tribals below poverty line who suffer from serious diseases like cancer, heart/kidney/brain ailments are the major components of the health care package. Construction of hospitals, mobile hospitals and mid-wifery centres in tribal belts and health insurance scheme for poor tribal families are also undertaken to promote tribal health.

The government has also implemented developmental schemes and plans for improving the social and economic status of tribals in the state. Need based and location specific packages emphasizing education, health and economic development of Adiyans, Paniyans and other socially and economically marginalized primitive tribal groups are introduced. The scheme for providing labour to the landless and financially unsound tribal families are implemented giving emphasis to land based activities for increased food production. Marriage of ST girls is also financially assisted. The housing schemes by the ST Development Department aim at providing financial assistance to houseless tribals to build houses. National Trade and Arts Festivals are organized to promote the exhibition and sale of tribals crafts and arts. Kudumbasree units are also extended to tribal areas to generate self employment opportunities among tribal women below poverty line. Measures are taken to organize Oorukootams in all tribal settlements at Grama Panchayat and Block Panchayat level for their empowerment. The scheme for resettlement of landless tribals includes development of minimum infrastructure needs including housing, agricultural development, self employment programmes, provisions for health care and skill development. Development plans for tribes living in forest provide employment to forest inhabited tribals and ensure alternative source of income, protection from wild animals, health care facilities and protection of local habitat. Special drinking water supply schemes are also implemented in the tribal belts of Idukki and Wyanad districts. The government also provide basic needs package consisting of shelter, water supply etc.

to the primitive tribal families of the state. The Indira Awaz Yojana, a centrally sponsored scheme provide houses to scheduled tribes. Another central scheme, the Swarna Jayanthi Gram Swarizgar Yojana envisages establishment of micro enterprises in the rural areas.

The government shows great interest in preventing the atrocities against the tribals of the state. Special benches have been constituted in all District Courts for the speedy disposal of cases registered under Prevention of Atrocities Act. Appropriate schemes are formulated to provide compensation and rehabilitation to the victims of atrocities and legally aid them.

The state government has set up an institution, KIRTADS, to conduct research, training and development studies on the scheduled castes and tribes of Kerala. The institution has three major wings viz, the Anthropologist Research Wing that undertakes research activities; the Training wing which conducts training programmes for officials and non officials and the Development Studies Wing which undertakes evaluation studies of various development programmes implemented for the benefit of the tribals. One of the major schemes under taken by KIRTAD is the Adikala Gramam scheme that encourages research on primordial arts and crafts forms and documentation of tribal arts and crafts. Annual grants are also awarded to promote master craftsmen, artists, musicians and kalasamithis.

Tribal development in Kerala has assumed greater significance in the context of the growing awareness among these people of their right place in the state's political scenario. But at the same time the tribals are made to suffer from exploitation, alienation from their land, disempowerment and exclusion. Even though the constitution and political leadership stood for positive measures for tribal development and empowerment, the insensitive and biased bureaucracy and administrative machinery tried their best to disempower the tribals in Kerala. It is a truth that the major political parties in Kerala have a vision on tribal empowerment. At the same time these parties and their leadership consciously closed their eyes on some crucial issues of tribal development and empowerment. The most vibrant among these issues is that of land alienation. The next chapter deals with the problem of the alienation of tribal land and the related approaches of the mainstream political parties of the state.

Notes and References

1. K. Panur, 2005, *Ente Hrudayathile Aadivasi* (Mal.) Kottayam, Current Books, p. 64.

2. Ibid. p. 65.

3. Mathrubhoomi Tozhil Vartha : Harisree 2006 (Mal.) Kozhikodu : Mathrubhoomi Publication, January 28, 2006, p. 4.

4. Dileep Raj, 2003, *Thantedangal : Kerala Samooha Bhoopatam Muthanga Samarathinu Sesham* (Mal.) Kottayam, D.C. Books, p. 62.

5. Ibid.

6. Mathrubhoomi Tozhil Vartha : Harisree, n. 3, p. 4.

7. Ibid.

8. Rajeevan. R., 2006. *Unveiling Injustice Towards Tribals : Kerala Scenario*, Indian Journal of Human rights and Social Justice, Vol. I, No. 1-2, pp. 53-61.

9. Dileep Raj, 2003, n. 4, p. 16.

10. Government of Travancore, 1948, *Acts and Proclamations of Travancore*, Travancore Government Press, Act II of 1068 (1903).

11. Ghanashyam Shah, 1990, *Socialist Movements in India – A Review of the Literature*, New Delhi, Sage Publications, p. 93.

12. Jaganath Pathy, 1987, *Tribal Peasantry – Dynamics of Development*, New Delhi, Inter-India Publications, p. 66.

13. Gavit, M.H. and Attar Chand, 1989, *Nehru : Tribal and Women Welfare*, New Delhi, H.K. Publishers & Distributors, p. 129.

14. Ibid, pp. 140-154.

4

Tribal Land Alienation: Political Empowerment Becomes a Compelling Necessity

Even after the promulgation of a democratic Constitution with its various provisions to safeguard the interests of tribal community, the tribals in Kerala could achieve no promising progress. The British alienated the tribals from their land and resources through the introduction of various land and tax policies. The British policies helped the immigrants and the planters to have access to tribal lands. The tribals were made to suffer from exploitation, alienation from their land, disempowerment and exclusion.

With the dawn of independence, the immigrants along with the insensitive and biased administrative machinery accelerated the process of disempowerment of the tribals in Kerala. It is a fact that after the second world war, with a vision of increasing agricultural production, the British and later the independent government of India encouraged agriculturists and farmers. In 1948, the Madras presidency introduced a scheme for ex-servicemen, by which it distributed forest land in Wayanad to ex-servicemen and some landless people including a few tribals.[1] The scheme was criticized as an anti tribal development scheme.

Agricultural settlers, mainly from central Travancore and Cochin who migrated to Palakkadu, Malabar and different parts of the western Ghats in the 1950s, was a great blow to tribal life. It should be noted that the tribals were poor, illiterate and suffered from indebtedness. Many of the immigrants had fraudulently alienated tribal land, exploiting the ignorance and innocence of the tribals.[2] The absence of tribal land laws to protect the tribal land, indirectly helped the immigrants to snatch tribal land by using various overt and convert methods.

Records say that among the tribal families in Kerala, 30% percent are landless. At the time of the formation of Kerala state, landlessness was least among tribals in Travancore and Kochi. The number of landless tribals remained low in Kottayam, Idukki and Thiruvananthapuram. The tribal sects of the region namely Kanikkar of Thiruvananthapuram, Malai Arayan of Idukki and Kottayam, Muthuvan of Idukki and Oorali of Idukki and Kottayam were the first to engage in systematic cultivation.[3]

It was in Malabar that the number of landless tribal families was high and that too in the districts of

Wayanad and Palakkadu. The Adiyas and Paniyas of the region who formed almost 27 percent of the tribal population in the state, remained landless for centuries. The large scale immigration of people especially from Travancore resulted in the tribals losing their agricultural land and hence their only means of sustenance. As the immigrants seized the tribal land through various means on a large scale, the tribals naturally became their slaves.[4] The most exploited tribal sects were Paniyas and Adiyas.

In Attappadi, immigration from the plains began in the 1950s. Within 25 years, 20 percent of the tribal families in the district were made landless. In the decade from 1966-1976, 44 percent of the tribal land in the district of Palakkad was seized by the immigrants. The mortaging of tribal lands too was higher in the district.

Both in the case of the cultivating land and in the case of average land possessed by each tribal family, the districts in the old Travancore-Kochi state stood ahead, while Malabar stood last.

Among the landed tribals, 62 percent of the families had an average of two acres of land in their possession. Since it was not adequate for their annual sustenance, they had to rely on labour work. 29 percent of the tribal farmers who possess 2-5 acres of land were small scale cultivators. That is 91 percent of the agriculturists among the tribals had to do other labours since the income from agriculture was insufficient for their livelihood. The percentage of families having land below 50 cents was also high in the Malabar region.

At present, the condition is worse than that prevailed thirty years back. Now more than half of the tribal population in Kerala (55.47 percent) is composed of landless agricultural labourers. The all India average is 32.99 percent. According to an estimate, the total land alienated until the end of 1996 is 80,590 hectares, of which only 440 hectares has been restored to the tribes.[5]

Land Reform Measures in Kerala

The first Communist government of Kerala (1957-59) enacted the 'progressive' land reforms law of Kerala, which was supposed to benefit the poorest and most marginalized groups like the tribals in the society. Even such a law was misused by the rich immigrants to alienate the tribals from their land. The tribals used to lease out their land for cultivation to the non tribal immigrants, who were considered tenants. According to the land reform law, the tenants would be entitled to get the land after a certain period of time and after paying nominal compensation. The rich immigrants gained the ownership of the leased land by eliminating the tribal land owner.[6] The fact that the immigrants cheated the tribals by making use of a law passed for the poor, is a clear example of how they are using political power and influence. On the other hand the tribals are neither organized nor powerful enough to resist such injustices.

The post independence development projects of Kerala also contributed much to the losing of adivasi land. The tribals lost 25924.315 hectares of land for the construction of dams, 2324.72 square kilometer for wild life sanctuaries and 182618.666 hectares for non forest purposes. (See the tables 5, 6 & 7 in the Appendices)

The land alienation issues of tribals were first addressed with the formation of the Dhebar Commission in 1960 by the Central government, which suggested that all lands alienated since January 26, 1950 should be restored. The R.Shankar ministry, which was then in power in the state of Kerala, has suggested to the Dhebar commission to include the tribal areas in Kerala in the list of scheduled areas.

The Kerala Government passed the Kerala Forest Act in 1961 to protect both the forest and forest dwelling tribals. The subsection (A) of section 76 of the Act empowered the state government to formulate rules for protecting and promoting tribal interests. Accordingly the Kerala Government published the Kerala Scheduled Tribes Rules in 1964.[7] It was upheld as highly beneficial to the tribal community of Kerala. It included adequate provisions for tribal development such as providing enough fertile land for cultivation free of cost, protection from the exploitation of intermediaries, adequate protection to them from exploitation etc. But a tribal belonging to Mala Araya caste and was a member of a co-operative society named 'Vana Mahasabha' challenged it in the High Court of Kerala. Actually he was becoming an instrument in the hands of vested interest who wanted to subvert the Rule. The Kerala High Court declared the subsection (A) of section 76 of the Kerala Forest Law null and void and the Kerala Scheduled Tribes Rule 1964 as illegal.[8]

As a result, the migrants got ample opportunity to alienate the tribals from their land in various ways including marrying tribal girls and thereby becoming owners of tribal land. The tribals were also supplied with liquor and loans as a means of snatching their lands from them.

On the recommendation of the Dhebar commission and on its endorsement by the Centre, the CPI led Achutha Menon government unanimously passed the Kerala Scheduled Tribes (Restriction on Transfer of Lands and Restoration of Alienated Lands) Act 1975.[9] This act (KST Act 1975) was further included in the ninth schedule of the constitution to ensure that the act by itself would not be challenged in any court of law.

The KST Act 1975 was significant in that it had acknowledged the inalienability of tribal land and the need for the restoration of alienated land. However, the rules and regulations accompanying the Act were not framed for many years. It was only in 1986 that the rules operationalising the Act was formulated.[10] According to this Act, all lands alienated from 1960 to 1982 had to be restored to the tribals and all such transactions had to be nullified. It also prohibited the transfer of lands from tribals to non tribals from January 1, 1982. Despite the restriction, the transfer of lands continued without any interruption. Figures indicate that the number of landless families increased from 3549 in 1976 to 22491 in 2001, a seven fold increase despite a ban on land transfer.[11]

As on 1991 there were 8553 applications submitted for restoration of 10,177 hectares of land. Later the number of applications rose to 8879.[12] Of these the maximum number of applications has come from the districts of Palakkad (2523) mainly from the Attapadi region and Wayanad (2229).[13] At the same time applications were filed in from almost all the districts of Kerala. Only 4,524 applications were accompanied by supporting evidences (which was necessary under the KST Act 1975) and therefore found valid. Accordingly, 3,170 hectares of land had to be restored.[14] Their ignorance of the alien concept of ownership coupled with an insensitive and biased administrative machinery that trivialized the traditional rights of the tribals, contributed to a situation where the tribals were left without valid proof of ownership or enjoyment.[15]

When the KST Act 1975 became a law in the year 1986, there was much opposition from the settlers and the officials showed only a lukewarm interest in implementing it. So the government of Kerala did almost nothing for the restoration of tribal land. So in 1988, Dr. Nalla Thampi Thera filed a public interest petition seeking the intervention of the Kerala High Court on the issue. The High Court issued an order on 15th October 1993 calling for the restoration of alienated land.[16] It also ordered the government to settle all cases relating to land alienation within six months of the issue of the order.

In 1996 the UDF government, through an ordinance tried to effect changes in the 1975 Act but the then Governor failed the attempt. A little later, the LDF government also tried the same but it too failed. Since the High Court of Kerala had issued a deadline that the alienated lands had to be restored by September 1996, the LDF government passed an amendment to the 1975 Act. On 23 September 1996, the Kerala state Legislative Assembly passed the Kerala Scheduled Tribes (Restriction on Transfer of Lands and

Restoration of Alienated Lands) Amendment Bill 1996[17] in the midst of opposition raised from various Human rights organizations and tribal organizations. The Bill provided legitimacy to tribal land transactions from 1960 to 1986, which was prevented in the original KST Act 1975. Accordingly the immigrants need not to restore the tribal lands occupied by them. Instead the new Bill proposed to restore equal area of land that they have lost elsewhere to the tribals along with an amount of Rs.25000 to each family. The tribal activists had made a representation to the President of India in this regard. The Bill proved to be the greatest injustice meted out by the state to its tribal subjects.

The tribal people expressed their protest in various forms. On October 4, 1996 the Ayyankali Pada detained Dr. W.R. Reddy, the District Collector of Palakkad for nearly nine hours as a sign of protest.[18] The amendment Bill which was sent to the President of India for his consent was rejected and returned by the Rashtrapathi Bhavan on March 1998.[19]

To escape from the pressure of tribal organizations and avoid criticism from judiciary, the Kerala Legislative Assembly passed "The Kerala Restriction on Transfer and Restoration of Lands to Scheduled Tribes" Bill on February 23, 1999 which was signed by the Governor of Kerala on March 9, 1999 and became a law.[20] The new Act made the KST Act 1975 invalid. According to the Act the immigrants need to return only tribal lands above 2 hectares. Lands below 2 hectares need not be given back to the tribals, instead they will be given equal area of substitute land elsewhere. The Bill further promises one acre of land to landless tribals in their own district within two years of its passing. Accordingly on 7 October 1999, the Kerala government started distributing lands to the tribals of Attappadi.[21] On 11 October 1999, the High Court of Kerala issued an order to stay the implementation of articles 5 and 6 of the Act, which allows substitute land for the alienated land.[22]

On 16 December 1999, the Division Bench of Kerala High Court which included Justice P.K. Subramanian and Justice C.S. Rajan pronounced its verdict that the Kerala government has committed contempt of court, while hearing a petition of contempt of court filed by Nalla Thampi Thera. Five more months were granted by the court to implement the KST Act of 1975. The court also warned the government that the Chief Secretary of the state will be punished in case the government fails to restore the alienated lands against which no case has been filed or no compensation has to be given, within five months. The Division Bench also made it clear that the Act of 1999 cannot pass over the Act of 1975.[23]

Politicisation of the Land Alienation issue and the move to empower the tribals of Kerala

The most peculiar feature of Kerala politics is the presence of two political coalitions – the Left Democratic Front (LDF) and the United Democratic Front (UDF). These two political coalitions monopolized the political power of the state. These two coalitions did very little to enforce the tribal protection laws effectively in the state. At the same time the tribals and dalit sections of Kerala are very active support structures to most of the political parties. But unfortunately, these political parties are indifferent towards the crucial issues of the tribal people.

When the tribal people lost their trust in the mainstream political parties, they extended their support to the Naxalite movement especially in Malabar areas. The Naxalite movement was strengthened in the Malabar areas mainly due to the irresponsible attitude of the mainstream political parties. It is also a truth that the Naxalite movement showed its power in the tribal belts of Kerala. The tribal people were enthusiastically attracted towards that movement. They believed that true attempts were made by the Naxalite movement to politically empower them. But the mainstream political parties were totally against the Naxalite movement for they realized the consequences of its growth. So the Government of Kerala discouraged the growth of the Naxalite movement through a suppressive policy. It was weaked with the assassination of its leader Varghese in a fake encounter with the police in February 1970.

Even though the mainstream political parties are indifferent towards tribal problems, they were very eager to have vote banks in tribal areas. That is why almost all the political parties have organized their tribal wings. The Adivasi Sangam organized by the Jan Sangh, Kerala Girivarga Sangam by the Communist party of India, Karshaka Sangam by CPI (M), Kerala Adivasi Samajam of Indian National Congress are some such examples.

The Wayanadu Adivasi Swayam Sevak Sangam (WASSS) was the first in this attempt. It was organized by the Jansangh in 1963 and was registered in 1969. A number of political programmes including Dharnas, picketing, satyagrahas were organized by this Sangam mainly for the restoration of their lost land. In 1969, a new Jan Sangh supported organization called 'Wayanadu Adivasi Sangham' was formed. It was mainly supported be the Kurichya sections of the tribal in Wayanadu.

The 'Karshaka Tozhilali Union' formed in 1963 with the support of CPI (M) mainly supported the farm workers who were in semi slavery. The organization conducted a number of struggles for establishing the rights of tribal agriculture workers. In 1975, the 'Kerala Girivasa Sangham' was also established with the support of the Communist Party of India. It was mainly organized with an intension of threatening out the immigrants from the tribal belt. But the organization ceased functioning by the proclamation of Emergency in 1975.

The Kerala Adivasi Samajam was formed in 1973 under the leadership of Indian National Congress. The Mulluva Kurumas were the strong support base of the organization. A number of political movements were conducted under its banner. They claim that the Central Government law of preventing slavery work and the State law for the restoration of tribal land were the results of their struggle.

A number of new tribal organizations emerged in different parts of Kerala within the last 25 years. They include Mala Araya Mahasabha in Idukki, Girijan Sevak Samithi in Attappadi, All Kerala Tribal Workers Union in Pathanamthitta, Adivasi Vikasana Pravarthaka Samiti, Adivasi Federation, Adivasi Aikya Samithi etc. in Wayanad and more recently the Adivasi Vimochana Munnani in Kannur. The Kerala Adviasi Samajam of

Indian National Congress, Vanavasi Kalyan Manch of the BJP and the CPI (M) led Adivasi Kshema Samiti are much influential among the tribals.

Tribal activism was present in some parts of the state under the banner of organizations like Naxalite movement, Ayyankali Pada etc. But tribal activism did not have any statewide impact. The Indian National Congress showed little interest in parochial issues related to the tribals. The left political parties, especially the Communist Party of India (Marxist), with which many tribal people had early association, saw the tribal question within a class frame work, and was not prepared to view it as a problem specific to certain communities. This universalizing stance of the leftists even on the tribal issues in Kerala was one of the reasons for the emergence of new tribal organizations like the Adivasi-Dalit Samara Samiti, the Adivasi Gothra Mahasabha and the Rashtriya Mahasabha.

The Naxalite movement and the Ayyankali Pada were known for its militancy and violence. A number of attempts were made to organize the tribals of Kerala in the model of People's War Group of Andra Pradesh. Even though the tribals in Kerala have unresolved problems, they realized these organizations as dangerous ones. That was the chief reason behind the weakening of such organizations. It was also the result of the political socialization of the tribals in Kerala in the right manner. It also empowered them to begin new methods of agitation based on democratic and peaceful means. For that they started politicizing the issue of land alienation of the tribals in Kerala.

One of the milestones in this regard is the eight day tribal meet held in October 1992 at Mananthavadi in the district of Wayanadu under the leadership of C.K. Janu. Tribal organizations from Kerala, Tamilnadu and Karnataka attended the programme. The meet discussed the various problems faced by the tribal in India. There was also an exhibition of tribal products, visit to tribal colonies and cultural fest in connection with the meet.

The meet gained significance as a movement of the tribals outside the banner of any of the mainstream political parties in the state. It evoked mixed reactions among the mainstream political parties and the public. The CPI (ML) and Bharatiya Janata Party conducted protest marches against it. At the same time, a few other organizations openly registered their appreciation for the meet. It was also alleged that the organizers of the meet received monetary help from abroad and had missionary interests.

The tribal meet of 1992 along with another meet in Kudak in Karnataka in 1993 inspired the tribal leaders to start a fresh movement to fight for their cause. Accordingly, they moulded action plans to give publicity and to bring public attention to the problems of land alienation especially to force the government of Kerala to implement the KST Act of 1975. Accordingly on Ist March 1994, the Collectorate of Wayanadu at Kalpetta was picketed under the leadership of Adivasi Samyukta Samara Samiti. They primarily demanded the restoration of their alienated land. On the same day another group of tribals under the leadership of Adivasi Aykya Samiti moved to Chingeli in Sultan Batheri and took hold of 528 acres of land. The land was proposed to be distributed among the tribals, though after four decades, the proposal remained unfulfilled. Following the two incidents a number of tribals were arrested and detained. The Adivasi Aykya Samiti conducted a strike by fasting for 48 days protesting against the atrocities of the police. Here also, the mainstream political parties kept silent without taking sides, though a number of dalit organizations supported the tribals.

Again on 3 April 1994, the tribals under another tribal organization, Adivasi Vikasana Samiti grabbed 128 acres of forest land at Ambukutty in Manantavadi (Wayanadu). This also resulted in police action and subsequently the tribal march to police station and strike by fasting. On 5 March 1995, there was another tribal movement to take hold of the Revenue land at Panaveli in Wayanadu. The tribals set up hamlets there and started farming. They were arrested and their hamlets were burned. But after an interval they again lay hold of the land.

Since the government of Kerala paid little heed to the problems of tribal land alienation, under the banner of Adivasi Ekopana Samiti, an awareness rally was organized from Panaveli in Wayanadu to Thiruvananthapuram in 22 days. On 26 February 1996, a group of tribal women under the leadership of C.K. Janu underwent a strike by fasting infront of Government Secretariat, Thiruvananthapuram. Supporting this a number of propaganda programmes were conducted in various district head quarters of the state. In the light of such developments, the then Chief Minister of Kerala invited the tribal leaders for a talk, which proved to be a failure.

On 23 September 1996, the then ruling LDF government of Kerala passed the Kerala Scheduled Tribes Amendment Bill, legitimizing the tribal land transactions from 1960 to 1986. The Bill was vehemently opposed by tribals all over Kerala. They adopted different means of protest such as fasting, processions, picketing at Secretariat etc. In October 1996, under the label of Ayyankalipada, the district Collector of Palakkadu, was detained for hours.

Another tribal organization Girijan Sevak Samiti observed 'black day' for 41 days at Attapadi in Palakkad to register their protest. The storm of protest could be calmed down only with the enactment of the Kerala Restriction on Transfer and Restoration of lands to Scheduled Tribes Bill of 1999. But the law was not enforced effectively.

The latest among the organizations formed for the empowerment of tribals in Kerala was the Adivasi Gothra Mahasabha, which came into being in 2001. It had an accidental origin. It was the outcome of many unfortunate starvation deaths among the tribals of Palakkad, Kannur and Wayanad districts in the year 2001. It demonstrated the hollowness of the achievements proclaimed by the state in terms of social micro-indicators. The organization made it clear that the tribals in Kerala have been largely kept away from the gains of the much vaunted 'Kerala Model of Development.'

The existing paradigm of development often resulted in seriously disturbing the tribal rights over their common property resources. This was possible because tribals across the state were, and are the least powerful interest group as well as the least powerful political force. On this issue, the tribals should be adequately socialized and empowered to fight for their resources – land, forest and water.

As a response to the deplorable condition of tribals, Kerala witnessed a non violent protest movement of the tribals demanding land, based on the premiss that it is lack of land that lies at the root of the tribal poverty. The tribal movement was led by C.K. Janu, a young neo-literate tribal woman born to a very poor Adiya tribal family in Wayanad, who was formerly a member of the Communist Party of India (Marxist). She led the struggle under the banner of the newly floated organization known as the Adivasi-Dalit Samara Samiti (ADSS). The movement began when C.K. Janu submitted an open letter to the Chief Minister of Kerala A.K. Antony on 24 August 2001. The protest strike of ADSS by setting up tribal huts on the premises of both the Government Secretariat and the Cliff House (the official residence of Chief Minister) had attained large scale attention of the press, intelligentia, officials and the people.

This was the first tribal movement in Kerala, which showed the unity and spirit of the tribals in the state. Almost all the tribal sections participated in the struggle. It had also believed to have gained moral support from almost all the communities of Kerala. The news as well as the spirit of this struggle spread to the tribal belts all over the state. It revolutionalised the tribal mindset of Kerala.

In the ADSS struggle the tribals raised demands, which nobody can neglect. They demanded five acres of land for each tribal family. Land was not seen only as a commodity with exchange value or as a status symbol. But it was also seen as connected with their culture, identity and also livelihood. Janu, their leader even identified the presence of certain spiritual elements in their land and the trees which tribals worship.[24] C.R. Bijoy correctly says: "Unlike others, tribals have a special relationship and dependence on land which gives them the notion of territoriality. Their existence as communities is possible only if their inalienable right to their territories is acknowledged."[25]

The ADSS struggle was noted for its peaceful and organized nature. The researcher feels that even the leaders of the movement were not fully optimistic of conducting such a struggle so organized and peaceful. During times of the researcher's interaction with various leaders of the tribals, they also described it as a milestone in proving the capability of tribal sections to conduct such struggles in future. The volunteers stated that their leaders trained them in such a way that they could conduct similar struggles. The leadership tactics attracted the intellectuals and the administrators of Kerala. It was for the first time that the tribal issues came to the forefront of the political agenda of Kerala.[26]

On the 48th day of the strike, that is on 16 October 2001, the Kerala government agreed the demands raised by the tribals. On the basis of the agreement, it was decided to grant five acres of cultivable land to each tribal family. In case if sufficient land was not available, each of them would be then given at least one acre of cultivable land. The activists of the ADSS largely laid emphasis on the distribution of forest land in Wayanad.[27]

The state government also agreed to recommend to the Centre to include tribal lands in the fifth schedule so that their land could not be alienated later. The state also assured that it would enact a law to prevent land grabbing and also make a master plan for creating jobs for their unemployed youths.

Among other important attempts, the protection of tribal land and culture and distribution of the land in the scheduled areas occupied a prominent position. The state planning board was told to prepare a master plan for integrated tribal development and to implement it on a time-bound basis from the very beginning of the tenth plan. All the projects under the TSP would hence forth run with an active participation of the tribals and the power of forest management would be taken away from the Forest Department and restored to the tribes.[28]

The tribal movement witnessed an unprecendented solidarity among various tribal groups in Kerala. The method of agitation was non-violent and it primarily targeted the state and in no way expressed hostility to the settlers. It is also noted that the Kerala government especially the then Chief Minister, A.K. Antony exercised restraint, inspite of pressures from various quarters, including political party leaders, to take tough stance for demolishing the illegally constructed huts in the Secretariat and Cliff House premises. He was also sympathetic to the tribal agitation and facilitated an early agreement on the land issue.[29] The agitation was described as a "moral booster for the tribal-dalit struggle across the country" and was acknowledged as the first successful democratic agitation demanding compensatory land against alienated tribal land. The most notable outcome of the agitation was that, they could form a new organization called the Adivasi Gothra Mahasabha during this period. The birth of that organization outside the mainstream political parties' framework was a land mark in the political empowerment of tribals in Kerala.

Notes and References

1. T.V. Achutha Varyar, 2003, *Gothra Sathyangal* (Mal.) Thrissur, Alter Media, pp.58-59.

2. There are several stories going round as to how the settlers, mainly Syrian Christians from Central Travancore, appropriated tribal land, particularly in Wayanad district. For example a provision shop owner from Central Travancore got five acres of cultivable land from a tribal on an agreement that the latter would be provided with salt from his shop free of charge until he dies, in lieu of the land transferred. There are also instances of land transfer for tobacco and country liquor. There are settlers who affirm the veracity of a number of such stories.

3. Dileep Raj, 2003, *Thandedangal: Kerala Samooha Bhoopadam Muthanga Samarathinu Sesham* (Mal.) Kottayam, D.C Books. p.17.

4. Ibid. p.18.

5. Government of Kerala (GOK) Department of Revenue 2001 c. *Administrative Report 2001*, Trivandrum, GOK.

6. T.V.Achutha Varyar 2003, n.1, p.47.

7. Government of Kerala (GOK) Notification No.M.S.575/64/ A.D. 19-8-1964, Trivandrum GOK.

8. Judgment of High Court of Kerala. 1970 KLT. 1069, Ernakulam HCK.

9. Government of Kerala, *Kerala Gazette (Extra-ordinary)* dated 14-11-1975 Notification No.673, Trivandrum, GOK.

10. Kerala Scheduled Tribes (Restriction on Transfer of Lands and Restoration of Alienated Lands) Rules 1986, *Kerala Gazette (Extra Ordinary) 934* dated 20-10-1986 G.O.(P) No. 730/86/RD dated18-10-1986.

11. Based on the comparison of data from the 1976 socio-economic survey of scheduled tribes and the Adivasi Master Plan Report of 2001.

12. Jose Chathukulam and M.S.John, "Issues in Tribal Development: The Recent Experience of Kerala", in Govinda Chandra Rath, (ed) 2006, '*Tribal Development in India: The Contemporary Debate*', New Delhi, Sage Publications India Pvt. Ltd, pp.182-2002.

13. Dileep Raj, 2003, n.3, p.21.

14. Ibid.

15. K.Kunhaman, 1985, The Tribal Economy of Kerala – An Intra-Regional Analysis, *EPW* XXX No.11, March 16, pp.466-74.

16. *Malayala Manorama* (Kottayam) October 16, 1993.

17. The Kerala Legislative Assembly, dated 23-9-1996. Bill.No.160 Trivandrum KLA.

18. *The Mathrubhoomi*, Kozhikode, October 5, 1996.

19. K.R. Narayanan was the President of India at that time. Since he belonged to the S.C. Section of Kerala, he could understand the situation of tribals in Kerala.

20. Government of Kerala, Notification No.22363/leg.A1/98/ Law dated 9-3-1999.

21. *Mathrubhoomi*, Thiruvananthapuram October 8, 1999.

22. Ibid, October 12, 1999.

23. Ibid, December 17, 1999.

24. *Madhyamam*, Thiruvananthapuram, October 28, 2001.

25. C.R. Bijoy 1999, Adivasis Betrayed: Adivasi Land Rights in Kerala, *Economic and Political Weekly* 29 May, Vol. XXXIV, No. 22, pp. 1329-35.

26. *The Hindu*, Chennai, October 19 & 20, 2001.

27. C.K. Janu and M.Geethanandan, 2001, *Adivasi Grama Panchayathum Swayambharanavum* (Mal.) Cochin, Clan n' Culture.

28. See the Interview of C.K. Janu by Zakkariah (a noted social critic in Kerala) in *Mathrubhoomi Daily* (June 2, 2002) entitled 'Adivasi Karar Attimarikkunnu' (Sabotage of the Deal with Adivasi).

29. *The Hindu*, Chennai, October 19, 2001.

5

AGMS and RMS: The New Experiments Towards Political Empowerment of Tribals in Kerala

The Adivasi Gothra Mahasabha (AGMS) was the child born out of the historical 47 days Adivasi-Dalit Samara Samiti (ADSS) agitation at Thiruvananthapuram. The organization later became an apex decision making body of the tribes in Kerala and fought for tribal interests across the state. It is the first all Kerala attempt to mobilize the tribals under an umbrella organization overcoming their differences. No doubt, the AGMS have provided tribal empowerment and politicization, a new dimension.

It was the first successful task to politically socialize the tribals in Kerala. In the AGMS the leaders of 33 clans of Kerala tribes were members. The leadership, recruitment and ideology of the organization (more exclusive compared to other previous mobilizations) were more endogamous, which provided the movement a form of social mobilization during its first phase, and later a form of politicization based on identity.

The ADSS agitation at Thiruvananthapuram generated a new spirit of unity in the minds of the tribals in Kerala. It strengthened the democratic ideals and political awareness among the tribals. It made them optimistic under a new leadership ie. C. K. Janu. All these together contributed the formation of a new tribal organization – the AGMS, an organization for fighting for the rights, liberation and empowerment of the tribals in Kerala.

With the signing of the agreement between Kerala government and ADSS, the first phase of its agitation came to a close. In that moment itself, a decision was taken by the leadership to begin a second phase of tribal agitation by strengthening AGMS. A strategy was formulated for that task. As part of this, the unsolved problems of tribals were analysed by visiting the tribal villages all over Kerala, and tribals were made conscious of the need and necessity to stay united in order to attain their rights. A strategy to socialize the tribal sections and to empower them was formulated.

Accordingly, young tribals were recruited as volunteers and necessary training and orientation were given to them to preserve the tribal diversity and protect their values. A self-reliant style of living was practiced by them to make the villages more autonomous. The tribal representative bodies (Uru Sabha) were restructured in that direction and strict codes of conduct were implemented to its members. The AGMS was strict in keeping liquor, tobacco, ganja and other intoxicating drugs away from the volunteers. The AGMS focused on bringing about external transformation at the individual level through individual regeneration by strictly insisting on observing the ethical codes. The tribals were made aware of the fact that, the life style of the tribals - addiction to drinks and drugs – directly and indirectly contributed to their cultural decay and disempowerment. The imposition of strict codes of conduct was a revolutionary policy of the AGMS.

The most distinguishing characteristic of AGMS was that it represented all the tribal people in Kerala, belonging to different gothras. The membership of gothras to the AGMS is decided on the basis of evaluation by the Gothra Mahasabha on social status and cultural level. While becoming a member of Gothra Mahasabha, each of these gothras retains the complete right to preserve their culture, language and tradition. Moreover each of these gothras has the right to maintain their own culture and rituals as well as to form organizations not only to preserve themselves but also to fight for their socio-economic rights. AGMS shall function as a common platform just to protect and promote the common interests of all tribal groups in Kerala. It was organized on the basis of strict democratic and federal principles. The leaders tried their best to avoid all types of controversies. The intention behind it was to tie them in a string without losing their distinct tribal identities.

AGMS – Composition

The AGMS is hierarchically organized with proper channels for enrolment and representation. Except the top stratum of AGMS, the lower levels follow the tribal pattern of organization.[1] The AGMS leaders visualized a loose federal arrangement for whole of the tribal segments through this organization. In various occasions, the AGMS leaders described it as an umbrella organization of the Adivasi gothras of Kerala.

Uru Sabha

Uru sabha shall function as the basic unit of AGMS. It may be organized by making its members, 25 or more families in a tribal settlement. If there are no sufficient members they can approach the nearest settlement in order to complete the tally. The Gothra Mahasabha members are elected from these Uru Sabhas. There will be at least two meetings of the uru sabha in a month and when an emergency situation arise, meeting may be convened at any time. Uru sabha is powerful enough to call back the elected members from the uru sabha to panchayat, district and state level, if they work against the interests of the uru sabha and the tribal community. The Uru Sabha is also empowered to elect new members in place of recalled members.[2]

Powers and functions of Uru Sabha[3]

1. To promote the socio-economic development of the tribal community in each of the settlements (uru) and to preserve its cultural identity and unity.

2. Each of the representatives of the uru sabha has the right to represent at various levels of government forums.

3. To interfere and represent all government sponsored development projects, the expenditure of funds and the selection of beneficiary for disturbing lands and determine whether land is cultivable or not.

4. To formulate tribal development projects for approval and implementation through the government sponsored development projects.

5. To determine the details of scheduled tribe areas and to ensure the leadership position of the Adivasi Uru Sabha in the formation of Adivasi Grama Panchayat.

6. To ensure the active participation and leadership of members of the Uru Sabha in the decision making process of the Adivasi Grama Panchayat in Scheduled Tribe areas.

7. To formulate the policies necessary for the re-establishment of lively relationship between nature, man and the forest resources.

8. To develop and transform the uru sabha into self governing institutions for the promotion of the socio-economic development of tribal community.

9. To formulate the laws necessary for the amicable settlement of all disputes between the members of the uru. If there are disputes (civil and criminal) which cannot be resolved at the level of uru sabha, the Gotra Sabha can interfere.

Panchayat Gothra Sabha (PGS)

Panchayat Gothra Sabha council consists of the representatives of the uru sabha in a panchayat. The PGS is directly responsible to the Gothra Maha Sabha and it would strive to implement the policy and programmes of the Gothra Maha Sabha. There shall be a panchayat presidium for the implementation of the decisions of the PGS. The presidium should represent the members of different tribal communities.[4]

District Gothra Sabha (DGS)

The district level Gothra Sabha comprises of the tribal Grama Panchayat and self-governing uru sabhas. It is the responsibility of the district Gothra Sabha to formulate the policy decisions in accordance with the aims and objectives of the state Gothra Sabha. To lead the various activities of the district level, there shall be a district level presidium from among the members of panchayat presidium. The membership of the district presidium should be equitably distributed among the various gothras. Women too should get due representation in DGS.[5]

State Presidium

The State Presidium of AGMS is a body comprising of tribal chieftains. The members of the State Presidium are nominated from the district presidium, which should represent all tribal sections in the district. While forming the State Presidium it should ensure that there are at least five presidium members from each district. This is intended to give adequate representation to those districts where the uru sabhas are few in number. The main function of the members of the State Presidium is to solve the problems of the tribals at various levels with the co-operation of governmental agencies.[6] The Gothra Mahasabha provided a practical form of direct democracy, to suit the modern life that has formulated from within the traditional tribal organizations. In the midst of several tribal organizations, the Gothra Mahasabha came up as a general assembly of the entire tribals in Kerala.

No doubt, the AGMS made a new history in the move to empower the tribal people of Kerala. Definitely the AGMS has provided the tribal politicization a new dimension. The general feeling is that it is an organization fighting for the general cause of tribals in Kerala with C.K. Janu as its leader. It is the first organization which has made genuine attempts to strengthen the tribals. C.K. Janu, a member of the Adiya community, from a very poor background and with no formal education, from the district of Wyanad has emerged as the undisputed leader of AGMS.[7]

C.K.Janu began her political career when she was recruited as a member of Karshaka Sangam affiliated to CPI (M). She later became a Panchayat member elected in the party ticket of CPI (M). She left the organization when she felt that the party did not give much importance to tribal issues especially the needs of its agricultural workers. Her emergence as a tribal leader articulating tribal questions especially the questions of power, land, property rights and self rule, revolutionized the process of tribal politicization and empowerment. The tribal movement under her leadership was strengthened at a time when the mainstream political parties and organizations failed to articulate the aspirations of the marginalised tribal sections of Kerala. It is believed that coalition politics leads to ideological compromises which also reduced the role of political left in the state to act radically for the tribal sections of Kerala.

The tribal struggle: From peaceful agitation to action oriented methods

The first organized agitation of the tribals of Kerala in a democratic and peaceful manner came to a close at Thiruvananthapuram with an agreement signed between Kerala government and the tribal leaders on October 16, 2001.[8] On the basis of the agreement, the Government of Kerala inaugurated the first land distribution at Marayur in Idukki district on time and it was inaugurated by the then Chief Minister of Kerala, A.K. Antony in the presence of tribal leaders.

Even though, the inaugural ceremony was conducted in a grant style, the government could not move ahead with the agreement. There was a serious allegation that the bureaucracy was deadly against the implementation of the agreement. Anyway, the state bureaucracy and its political leadership could not implement the provisions of the agreement. The report of the Government of Kerala sent to the National Human Rights Commission (NHRC) in April 2002, states that 568 families had been provided 1,308 acres of land since 1 January, 2002, the day on which the programme was inaugurated. Only 1.06 percent of the families have been provided 2.2 percent of the identified land within the first four months of the stipulated 12 month period.[9] Since then there has not been any substantial or significant change in these figures except that the land actually allotted has been reported in the media as

1,746.62 acres to 834 families. Only three percent of the promised land has been allotted in a year.[10] Also the rate of allotment has gone down drastically as only around 434 acres have been distributed from April 2002 to February 2003 as compared to the over 1,300 acres in the first four months.[11] This shows the irresponsibility on the part of the government to distribute land to the landless tribals of Kerala.

There are also a number of evidences, which show the hidden agenda on the part of the Kerala government to implement the agreement. In May 2002, the head of the tribal mission was quietly replaced by a forest official of the government's choice. The lands identified for distribution plummeted from 59,452 acres to a mere 2,300 acres in June 2002 and further to 1,223 acres when it came to the hands of the cabinet sub committee. That the adivasis have prior claims to most of these lands before these were declared state property in a historical point, has been conveniently glossed over. Instead it almost appears as if the lands are being bestowed by the state on the adivasis out of sheer generosity. Another major hurdle is said to be that a large portion of lands identified earlier are actually disputed land with the forest department and revenue department or are in the process of being confirmed as reserved forests, and that Forest Conservation Act 1980 stands as a legal hurdle in the way of identifying and transferring these lands to the tribals. This is totally misleading and is a gross misrepresentation of legal facts and the rights of tribals on forest.[12]

The AGMS represented these issues to the Government of Kerala. The organization, through various platforms including media, corner meetings etc. tried to make the issue live. But at the same time it could not make any strong impact on the government, and the crucial tribal issue have remained largely unfulfilled. This forced the tribal leaders to think of an alternative method of struggle for the accomplishment of their basic demands. It was alleged by the AGMS that the existing politico-administrative arrangement failed to uphold the KST Act, 1975 by its unwillingness to implement it. Even though both the ruling coalitions – the LDF and the UDF – had enough time to implement the act, both of them showed an indifferent attitude to the issue.

The AGMS and its leaders realized the fact that, the democratic and peaceful method of petitioning is not at all sufficient to protect and promote the interests of the tribals in Kerala. It required a popular uprising to challenge and force the state to come to terms with the injustice. It was against such a backdrop that the AGMS took matters into its own hands by a symbolic and pragmatic move. On January 4, 2003 after the deadline prescribed by the government expired on Dec. 31, 2002, the AGMS under the leadership of C.K. Janu and M.Geethanthan entered into the deforested portions of the Muthanga and its vast eucalyptus plantations.[13] It was a protest movement against the Government of Kerala which violated the agreement that land distribution would commence on January 1, 2002 and be completed on December 31, 2003. It was also agreed that a proposal based on the Cabinet decision to include Adivasi areas in the schedule V would be sent to the centre for further notification. This was to enable the tribals to enjoy the provisions of the Panchayat Raj

(Extension of Scheduled Areas) Act 1996 that provides for elements of self-governance.[14]

The Muthanga entry was not a decision taken in a fine morning. The programme was evolved out of widespread discussions and consultative process all over the state's tribal belt. In the consultative process the AGMS expressed its commitment to bring the agreement into effect at any cost. This participatory democratic process culminated in a huge gathering of thousands of tribals all over the state at Mananthavady in Wayanad district on August 25, 2002 when a 60 member tribal court (20 women and 40 men) representing different tribal communities was constituted. The tribal court declared once again that in view of the non-implementation of the 'agreement', the Adivasi shall establish their right by occupying the lands.[15]

The fact remains that, the decision to enter into the Muthanga land was the decision of the Gothra Mahasabha, which is the General Assembly of the entire tribals in Kerala. The Gothra Mahasabha with the support of tribals all over Kerala organized and led the Muthanga Agitation. Here lies the relevance of the Muthanga episode in Kerala's political scenario.

The Government of Kerala considered it as a unilateral decision of the Gothra Mahasabha and paid less interest to solve the problem amicably. So there was no serious discussions made. At the same time, the government faced different types of pressures from various quarters to suppress the tribal movement. On February 19, 2003, the state suppressed the move through police action.[16] Serious allegations were made against the tribal's movement including their links with PWG of Andhra Pradesh and even the LTTE of Sri Lanka. Chief Minister A.K. Antony, revealed that the tribals had plans to take his ministers hostage; the hit list later expanded to IAS and other officers as well as the foreigners who had come to Kerala to attend the Global Investors Meet (GIM).[17]

The fact that the agitation was brutally suppressed and the participants including its top leaders like C.K. Janu and Geethanandan were arrested and tortured inside the jail, never put out the spirit of the struggle. The forty four day's republican life at Muthanga inspired those stayed there a lot.

The people who stayed at Muthanga explained their experience as a unique one. They lived together in peace and harmony there. The most important feature of the life at Muthanga was that it could minimize the practice of untouchability still prevailing among some tribal sects. Further they could successfully implement total prohibition of liquor which was a bane on tribal life. Though they couldn't attain the professed aim of gaining land, the agitation instilled the spirit of renaissance in the hearts of the tribals of the state. It proves to be a milestone in the path of political empowerment of the tribal sections in Kerala.

It is a truth that, the inhumane police actions and the human rights violations on the marginalised sections of Kerala made serious impact on them. The antipathetic attitude of the two major political fronts in Kerala reveals their apprehension for the emergence of a people's movement outside themselves.

The tribal sections of Kerala was a strong support base to most of the political parties of Kerala in their area. History shows that the political parties also utilized the tribals for their political gains. But it is unfortunate that these political parties ignored tribals, when it came to the question of democratizing the power structure and their socio-economic upliftment. As a result the tribals continue to remain outside the power-structure and increasingly becoming marginalized and disempowered. From this disempowerment, started the process of disempowerment under the banner of AGMS and under the leadership of C.K.Janu.

The tribals in Kerala realized through the Muthanga incident that without political power, their socio-economic needs and aspirations will not be realized. The AGMS conducted a 'Muthanga Samara Sandesha Yathra' under the leadership of C.K. Janu to make the Kerala society aware of the political importance of Muthanga struggle, inhuman police actions and human rights violations. It mainly intended to the unification and empowerment of the tribals and dalits across the state. C.K. Janu, in the concluding session of Muthanga Sandesha Yathra rally in Thriuvananthapuram, noted that the greatest achievement of the Muthanga struggle was that it could make the Adivasi community politically conscious. The Adivasis realized that their problems required political solutions and not sympathetic approaches.[18]

The leaders of the AGMS declared that they realized the necessity of forming a political organization for the fulfillment of their long cherished goal of political empowerment. They also realized the fact that the tribals constitute only one percent of the total population of Kerala. So they decided to accommodate the non-unified and non-empowered dalits along with them. The search for such a political polarization finally got crystallized in the name of Rashtriya Maha Sabha (RMS).

The tribal sections in Kerala mostly believe that their concerns will never be sympathetically taken care of by the political parties. The mainstream political parties of Kerala take up the issues of tribals as some among the many issues they handle. Even the activists of political parties admit it. They favour the unification of the tribals of Kerala under a powerful political or non political organization constituted for the cause of tribals. The growth of Adivasi Gotra Maha Sabha resulted from such a vision. The AGMS, with in a very limited period, became the most powerful organization of tribals in Kerala.

The AGMS was the first tribal organization in Kerala, which come forward with the burning issues of land alienation and presented it before the social and political dais of Kerala in a grand manner. The organization tried to draw the attention of the Government of Kerala and the Kerala public to their problems in a different manner. Above all they could rise the tribal issues of Kerala at national and international levels. The tribals of Kerala considered AGMS as a great phenomenon and whole heartedly supported it. It was also important because their struggle had come to a close with the signing of an agreement with the government of Kerala. The leaders of AGMS, especially C.K. Janu, was lauded by the tribals all over Kerala irrespective of their caste and politics. The name of the organization because more popular with the Muthanga struggle.

While explaining the significance of AGMS, nobody can ignore their vital contributions. First of all, the AGMS could bring the land alienation issue in its real spirit to the notice of the government of Kerala, conduct memorable struggles for the cause and above all could make the public aware of the burning issues of tribal in Kerala. Secondly it led the first tribal movement for the cause, which came to a close with a written agreement with the government regarding the releasing of lands to them. This organization could effectively convince the government the truth that it is the lack of sufficient land that lies at the root of all the tribal problems.

The formation of AGMS had definitely offered a chance to the tribals of Kerala to organize themselves under a platform and thereby to raise their demands, and struggle for its fulfillment. Before the initiatives of AGMS, the Kerala public was less aware of the problems of these marginalized sections of people living in remote hills and its valleys. The organization could successfully propagate how the tribals were exploited by the people of the mainland and how much they were alienated from their traditional land. The AGMS also displayed how to organize the tribals in a systematic manner and how to organize struggles and to make it result oriented. Above all at least it could kindle a light towards the organization of tribal in Kerala in a broad way irrespective of their caste, religious, regional and lingual diversities.

The research study also reveal the limitations and short comings of the organization. While admitting its achievements a number of respondents pointed out its associations and weaknesses. First of all AGMS was centered in the district of Wayanadu and in certain tribal sects only. The failure of the organization to have influence in other places of Kerala is definitely a short coming of AGMS. The researcher noticed the indifferent attitude of the respondents of other districts towards AGMS. It has neither organizational roots nor programmes in other places, even if there is, it is only in a limited scale. It must have its branches, atleast one in all the districts. Since it has no organizational network in tribal concentrated areas, it cannot take up the diverse issues of the tribal sects all over Kerala.

Considering the above mentioned inadequacies of AGMS, one would automatically raise questions like whether the AGMS could bring the various tribal organizations functioning all over Kerala under an umbrella or what the approach of tribal people working in various political parties will be towards such a unity. The experiences all over the world shows that it is difficult to materialize such a dream. The AGMS also tried its best to shape a federation of tribal all over Kerala, but nothing materialized so far. With the formation of Rastriya Maha Sabha, the mission faced new challenges.

Rashtriya Maha Sabha (RMS)

The AGMS played a successful role in the political socialization of the tribal people of Kerala. It further thought that it is imperative to have a powerful political organization to articulate the aspirations of the tribal community. Rashtriya Maha Sabha came into being at Ernakulam on 19 February 2004.[19] The members of the AGMS and of forty Dalit organizations elected C.K. Janu as the President and M. Geethanandan as the General Secretary of RMS. The RMS consists of a state council of Uru Sabhas, the communal and service organizations of Dalits, Dalit Christians and other communal groupings and labour guilds. The representatives of all these sections constitute the state council which in turns selects the Secretariat.[20] The formation of RMS opened a new chapter in the polarization of tribal and marginalized sections of Kerala with a belief that political power is a crucial component, which can be achieved by capturing a share of power in state governance.

It is true that the transformation of the tribal movement into a political movement in Kerala is definitely a positive step towards their political empowerment. But while AGMS was a solidarity of tribals alone, the new political organization formulated out of it, RMS, coopted the other marginalized sections including the dalits and dalit Christians for strength and mass base. As such, it is doubtful whether the broader move will be beneficial to tribal unity and empowerment. It is also not clear whether the tribals can preserve the traditional cultural, social and economic systems with in such an organization or can retain their dominance in it. Further, the other sections in it may not participate in strikes particularly pertaining to tribal issues. In such an organization there may arise differences of opinion between tribals and others while shaping decisions, political goals and strategies. The fact that the other sections like Dalit Christians have a political base and support too affects the smooth functioning of the organization. On the other hand, the reservations of seats in PRIs, special developmental schemes and fundings for tribals would leave the other sections discontented. It is also doubtful whether the organization is based on any ideology or has been merely formulated for vested interests. Also the organization is yet to prove that it is a political party rather than a mere pressure group. In the political context of Kerala where only two political fronts come to power alternatively, RMS can become a decisive political force only if it is able to bring the whole tribal belt under their banner and share power in state government by making alliance with either of the political fronts. These are issues to be pondered over and overcome, before RMS could become a powerful political force in the state. However AGMS and RMS through their programmes and activities have inculcated social awareness into the mind set of the tribal community in the state and thereby accelerated the process of their political socialization.

Notes and References

1. The Constitution of AGMS, 2002, published by AGMS, p.3.
2. Ibid. p.5.
3. Ibid. p.6.
4. Ibid. p.8.
5. Ibid.p.10.
6. Ibid.p.11.

7. Bhaskaran, 2003, *'Janu' Biography,* Kottayam, D.C. Books.

8. *The Hindu*, Thiruvananthapuram, October 17, 2001.

9. C.R.Bijoy, K. Ravi Raman, 2003, *Muthanga – The Real Story: Adivasi Movement to Recover Land*, Economic and Political Weekly, Vol. XXXVIII No. 20 May 17, 2003.

10. Ibid.

11. Ibid.

12. P.K.Prakash, 2004, *Muthanga Vaarshikathil Uyarunna Chodyangal*, Madhyamam Weekly, February 27.

13. *Mathrubhoomi*, Thiruvananthapuram, January 5, 2003.

14. B.D. Sharma, 2003, *Self Rule Laws*, Thrissur, Alter Media Publications, p. 64.

15. C.K.Janu, M.Geethanandan, 2003, *Muthangayilekkulla Thirichupokku – Oru Sathyavangmoolam*, Published by AGMS.

16. *Malayala Manorama*, Thiruvananthapuram February 20, 2003.

17. *The Hindu*, Thiruvananthapuram February 27, 2003 & The Indian Express, Thiruvananthapuram, March 1, 2003.

18. *The Hindu*, Thiruvananthapuram, June 1, 2003.

19. Ibid, February 20, 2004.

20. *The Indian Express*, Thiruvananthapuram, March, 1, 2004.

6

The New Panchayati Raj System: A Shift Towards Improved Participation and Empowerment of Tribal Community in Kerala

Panchayati Raj Institutions, particularly in a developing country like India endeavouring to operate a democratic system of government, can play a vital role in the process of political legitimization and political development. It also ensures the participation of the people in the development process of the state. Involvement of people in the development process has been considered as the most effective means through which political, economic and social development can meet the aspirations of the people and to ensure that the benefit really percolate down to the lowest strata of the society. There has always been the feeling that Panchayati Raj Institutions (PRIs) are the most suitable agency for democratic decentralization, which could be equipped with adequate powers and responsibilities so that they could formulate and implement programmes of development.

Panchayati Raj bodies, which are genuine and effective democratic decentralized institutions, provide ample opportunities for a large number of rural people to take genuine and effective participation in the development and democratic decision making process. It helped to infuse in the minds of the rural people a spirit of self help, self dependence and self reliance and to gain experience in the art of social self government.[1]

Mahatma Gandhi was the champion of democratic decentralization and village autonomy. His concept of village panchayat as an instrument for the management of a village as a self governing and self sufficient entity in matters of basic needs as well as the exercise of such functions that can ensure the growth of village as an agro industrial community. Preservation and promotion of the resources of all kinds of a village community is solely the responsibility of the community as a whole. Gandhiji wrote: "Independence must begin at the bottom. Thus every village will be a republic or Panchayat having full powers. It follows therefore, that every village has to be self-sustained and capable of managing its affairs to the extent of defending itself against the whole world."[2] By this Gandhiji emphasized both the political and economic aspects of decentralization.

Gandhiji's approach to democratic decentralization starts from the bottom, where the people are free to formulate their policies and implement them without any rigid or strict control of the higher authorities or their frequent interference in day to day functioning.

Democratic decentralization is one of the media of people's participation and empowerment. The direct participation of the people in democracy at the grass root level would mark the shift in their participation from representative democracy to that of participatory democracy.[3] Democratic decentralization implies people's right to initiate their own projects for local well being and exercise their power to execute and operate them in an autonomous manner. The idea of democratic decentralization is just an extension of people's right to manage their own affairs in local areas without any undue interference from regional or national authorities. In short democratic decentralization emphasises people's participation and autonomy.[4]

From the dawn of Indian independence, attempts were initiated to attain the Gandhian concept of decentralized and autonomous village republics. For that purpose Article 40 was incorporated in the Constitution of India which directs the state governments to organize village panchayats and endow them with such powers and authority as may be necessary to enable them to function as units of self government.[5] Another milestone in this direction was the shaping of a view point relating to the implementation of five year plans in such a way that people's participation would be promoted in the management of rural development through local representative institutions.[6] With such an intention, number of studies were made and commissions were appointed. But only some of the reports were partially implemented and others were freezed for ever.

However, the contribution of Prime Minister Nara Simha Rao was unique in this regard. His government enacted a legislation in such a direction in 1992, through the 72 and 73 amendment Bills. On December 22, 1992, the Constitution Amendment Bill on Panchayati Raj was passed by the House of people and the next day by the Rajya Sabha giving Constitutional status to the rural local self governments.[7] The Act came into force with effect from 24 April 1993. The Act authorizes the state governments to make and pass necessary legislations according to their convenience. Based on the central Act the U.D.F government in Kerala has also given shape to a legislation called Kerala Panchayati Raj Act 1994.

As per the new legislation, elections to the local Panchayati Raj bodies were conducted simultaneously in the three tiers and a new blood of representatives took office by 1995. It was in this context that the LDF government which came to power in the state in 1996 initiated a new phase of decentralized planning. It was decided to devolve 35-40 percent of the State's 9th plan outlay for projects and programmes drawn up by the local self government. It was also decided to shape the 9th plan as a People's plan. It aimed at transforming the centralized planning to a decentralized one and to revive the participatory spirit and thereby ensure empowerment of the bottom layers of the society.

In view of the weakness of the satisfactory implementation of the Tribal Sub Plan (T.S.P),[8] during the 9th five year plan in connection with the decentralization of power and people's plan programme, the Panchayat Raj institutions were given the power and responsibility to implement the TSP. $^2/_3$ share of the TSP had been handed over to the PRIs. In view of the 'weakness of tribal movements, organized trend of the settlers and past experience,' it was decided to vest the major share of the funds with the District Panchayat.[9] Accordingly, the allocation for the district was 60 percent, with 20 percent each for the Gram and Block Panchayats.

It was decided to utilize the tribal fund effectively and vigilantly. For that purpose a district level committee was constituted with MLAs, members of the District Panchayats from SC/ST communities, senior officials and prominent social workers who were behind the formulation and implementation of various development programmes for the weaker sections. The Committee was empowered to enquire into any allegation concerning the TSP. A special task force chaired by the ST member to over see the drafting of the TSP was also envisaged. The sectoral guideline under the decentralized plan campaign, that a minimum of 40 percent should be set apart for the productive sector, was relaxed for the TSP, recognizing that the tribals were lagging behind in the economic and entrepreneurial fronts. However, the ceiling of 30 percent on the infrastructure sector was insisted upon.[10]

Even though there was committees and task force, these were not adhered to in practice.[11] In the Panchayat Development Reports, there was a chapter on SCs and STs, which did not amply reflect the needs and status of these segments. There have been instances of prejorative remarks about the tribals and dalits finding a place in the chapter on SCs and STs in the development reports of several Panchayats, leading to protest and in some cases even the burning of the development reports.[12] Persons from other communities were unwilling to participate in the SC/ST subject group either in the Grama Sabha or in the development programmes. When infrastructural projects were prepared, maps, as had been stipulated, did not accompany them. The majority of the districts do not have district level monitoring committees. Even in those places were these were constituted, this was done late. These committees were not convened regularly and had failed to monitor the TSP projects. The provision that the committee could enquire into allegations about the TSP did not actually take place any where in Kerala. Like wise, there had been no special project appraisal in respect of TSP projects before they were approved. Hence most of these rules remained merely on paper. Further the methodology for devolution, with the larger share of the TSP being given to District Panchayat did not produce the expected results.[13]

After a year of planning a cadre of educated tribal youth, described as social workers, has been appointed since it was found after finding that the participation of the tribals in the planning process was lagging behind. These social workers who were paid a monthly honorarium, were expected to call tribal neighbourhood gatherings (Urukuttams) and harness people's participation in the planning process in the tribal areas. The task of the social workers, who are called tribal promoters, was to visit the Uru kuttams, inform the people about government programmes and ways of accessing them and organize neighbourhood meetings.

The issues raised in such meetings were to be brought to the attention of the Grama Sabha and the Panchayat. They were given a five day intensive training at the time of appoinment. It may be noted that the tribal promoters were positioned in the ITDP office and not attached with the Panchayat, even though they were deployed in every Gram Panchayat having a sizeable tribal population.[14] A number of these tribal promoters were later contested in panchayat elections and some of them are elected and became tribal representatives at PRIs.

After considering the defects of the TSP implementation through PRIs, the UDF government reversed it to the old practice and placed the TSP at the disposal of the Director, Scheduled Tribes Development Department, through an order issued in October 2001. However it was stipulated that before projects were taken up the urukuttams should be convened in all wards of the Grama panchayats which have a population of more than 50 tribals. In the case of wards having a population of less than 50, such meetings could be organized at the Panchayat level. In formulating the infrastructural projects, the advice of the urukuttams is sought especially, in major activities like spot selection and preparation of social maps. The urukuttam was empowered to conduct social audit of schemes.

But after two years, the same government re-examined the operation and functioning of the scheme. On the basis of this, in the year 2003-04, the government gave back half the amount of TSP to the PRIs. The objective behind the transfer of the responsibility of implementing Tribal Sub Plan to PRIs are given as follows.

1. To ensure the empowerment and participation of tribal society.
2. To formulate the schemes taking into consideration their living conditions and life styles.
3. For effective and participatory planning.
4. To put an end to corruption and loss of resources through transparent execution.
5. To achieve social progress through effective monitoring.

The Government of Kerala issued a detailed guideline as per the Government Order (MS) 54/2003/ Planning, for preparing a comprehensive and effective Tribal Sub Plan avoiding limitations in the developmental strategies implemented during the IXth plan. It focuses on the following issues:

1. To give opportunity to the tribal sections to express their opinions on matters relating to the developmental programmes meant for them.
2. To strengthen urukuttam to provide the opportunity to take decisions positively.
3. To provide the tribals with key power in the utilization of resources set apart for tribal welfare.
4. To carry out tribal enforcement in its real sense.
5. To improve the quality of planning.

However studies and statistics reveal that the Panchayati Raj Institutions in Kerala has not imbibed the essense of this guideline and hence has not succeeded in successfully carrying out the Tribal Sub Plan.

The new Panchayati Raj Institutions are established with an intension to formalize and strengthen the democratic system especially among the under privileged. As far as the tribal sections of Kerala are concerned, it provided an opportunity to constitute a formal self government for them. The establishment and strengthening of self government offered enough opportunities to the tribal people towards political participation and empowerment. The urukuttam and Grama Sabha offered them an opportunity to formulate and implement schemes and programmes to meet their social needs, to mobilize people, to chanalize their energies towards socio-economic reconstruction and to involve them in all the activities of their communities through their own forums. The urukuttam and Grama Sabha are the pivots of decentralized governance and became vibrant and important institutions at the grass root level. It is a truth that collective and responsible mode of working of the urukuttam and Grama Sabha would be a more reliable vehicle of good governance than a relatively encumbered bureaucracy or locally elected representatives. As observed by Malini Nambiar, "it is certain that unless we have a vibrant Grama Sabha, we cannot have empowered and accountable panchayats.[15]

The introduction of the new Panchayati Raj system with provision for Urukuttom and Grama Sabha in tribal areas definitely accelerated the processes of political socialization and participation more than ever. It directly and indirectly helped the tribals to achieve a number of gains. The chief among those achievements are the following.

1. Fifty percent of the amount allotted for TSP was utilized through Panchayati Raj Institution as proposed by the tribals.

2. Through the formation of Urukuttam, the participation of tribals was increased.

3. The reservation of seats in the three tier Panchayati Raj System enabled them to shape a tribal political leadership and they got an opportunity to contest and win in elections.

4. The new PRI provided training to the tribal leadership in the governance process of formulation and implementation of plans and schemes.

5. Through the participation of tribals, there emerged new chances of formulating policies by realizing the real needs of the tribals.

But even after one decade of its experience, the Panchayati Raj system could not achieve its major goal of the empowerment of tribal sections of Kerala in its real spirit. The chief reasons behind it are

1. The guidelines issued by the state were not followed properly.

2. Tribal sub plan amount allotted to panchayats were not fully utilized.

3. The priority orders of developmental schemes were violated. Instead over importance was given to infrastructure development.

4. Urukuttam meetings were not conducted as per the guidelines. They were done in a perfunctory manner with out proper preparations.

5. The decisions of the Urukuttam meetings were subverted.

6. Working groups were not formulated by assuring adequate participation of tribals.

7. Absence of Scheduled Tribe promoters and the lack of interest on the part of officials and lack of training programmes for the elected representatives adversely affected the proper conducting of Urukuttam.

8. Proper initiative was not taken to develop thrust in the tribals on decentralized planning and local governing bodies.

9. Monitoring system did not come into existence and training was not given in social auditing.

If the authorities show a little more interest, a number of these defects may be rectified. But at the same time they are facing a number of other problems which cannot be easily rectified. The major problems that the tribal sections of Kerala face in general in the way of their socialization, participation and empowerment are as follows:

1. Acute poverty.

2. Negation of rights.

3. Alienation in socialization and developmental processes.

4. Lack of social, economic and political empowerment.

5. Repurcussions of exploitation in production and distribution system.

6. Negation of opportunity in gaining rights.

7. Under participation in decision making process on issues related to development.

8. Exploitation of intermediate in developmental programmes.

9. Rapid alienation of properties including land.

10. Declining of conventional social system and leadership.

11. Tendency to be an instrument in the hands of mafias who are engaged in crimes like forged liquor making, ganja planting, robbing valuable forest resources etc.

12. Formulating temporary and inflexible developmental programmes without proper scientific planning.

13. Tendency to create a dependent attitude by giving concessions rather than implementing schemes to improve efficiency.

From the study it is suggested that the Urukuttams and Grama Sabhas should be strengthened. There should be effective measures to safeguard and preserve the traditions and customs of the tribal people. The positive aspects of their traditional styles might be rejuvenated to strengthen Urukuttam and Grama Sabha. For example their traditional leadership styles should be promoted by giving them important portfolio in Grama Panchayat for cultural identify and customary mode of dispute resolution. Another suggestion is that sufficient number of ST promoters should be appointed and improve their efficiency through proper training. Their service should be strengthened among the forest dwelling tribal sects. Training to the ST promoters should be meaningfully and effectively made by availing the faculty and resources of institutions like IMG, KILA and KIRTHADS. Effective training should also be extended to elected tribal representatives, working group members, members of social service organizations, CDS representatives and officials of the ST Development department.

To conclude, the reservation of tribals in PRIs is a great milestone in the political socialization, participation and empowerment of tribal people in Kerala. But at the same time we cannot ensure tribal empowerment just by providing reservation facility and increasing the number of tribal representatives in the PRIs. There is an urgent need to opt for an effective device whereby maximum number of that section were made aware and motivated to come forward for active participation for the proper implementation and execution of Panchayati Raj System in tribal areas.

The next chapter details the attitude of common tribals towards Panchayati Raj Institutions, Urukuttams, Grama Sabhas and related issues.

Notes and References

1. Ratna Ghosh and Alok Kumar Pramanik (ed.), 1999, *Panchayat System in India: Historical, Constitutional and Financial Analysis,* New Delhi, Kanishka Publishers pp. 31-40.

2. M.K. Gandhi, 1953, *Village Swaraj* (completed by H.M. Vyas) Ahemadabad, Navjeevan Publishing House, p.3.

3. Shrawan Kumar Singh, 1993, *Building up of Peoples Institution* Article in the Journal of Kerala Institute of Local Administration, Thrissur, p.31.

4. Iqbal Narayan, 1981, *The Idea, the Image and the Reality in Panchayati Raj,* Delhi, Indian Institute of Public Administration, pp.13-14.

5. *The Constitution of India,* Part IV, Article 40.

6. B.S. Khanna, 1996, *Panchayati Raj in India: Rural Self Government,* New Delhi, Deep and Deep Publications, p.6.

7. J.Prabhash, 1995, *Panchayati Raj* (Malayalam) Thiruvananthapuram, Kerala State Resource Centre, p.22.

8. In the post independent India several plans have been implemented by the centre as well as the state governments for the development of the tribal community. The tribal sub plan was implemented from 1975 for the wholesome development of the tribal areas. But till the 8th five year plan tribal schemes were not satisfactorily executed due to the limitations of centralized planning. The tribal people could avail themselves of only a small

percentage of the benefits of the developmental schemes implemented during that period.

9. Thomas Issac 2000. *Local Democracy and Development.* New Delhi Leftward Publishers, p.160.

10. Ibid. p.162.

11. Jos Chathukulam, C.V. Balamurali and K.N. Jayan, 2000. *Study on special component plan and tribal sub plan under decentralized planning process in Kerala*, Kottayam, Centre for Rural Management.

12. Jos Chathukulam and M.S. John, "Issues in Tribal Development: The Recent Experience of Kerala" in Govinda Chandra Rath (ed) 2006. *Tribal Development in India: The Contemporary Debate*, New Delhi, Sage Publications, pp.182-202.

13. Ibid.

14. Ibid.

15. Malini Nambiar 2001. *Making the Grama Sabha Work,* Economic and Political Weekly, Mumbai, August 18.

7

Political Socialization and Political Participation of Tribal Community in Kerala: A Face to Face Analysis

This chapter examines the attitude of the tribal people of Kerala towards politics in general. It makes an attempt to highlight the political behaviour of the tribal people, which reveals the level of their political socialization, participation, empowerment and related issues.

The study is essentially based on primary data collected from a cross section of tribal people belonging to four districts of Kerala – Thiruvananthapuram, Kollam, Palakkad and Wayanad. From these four districts eight panchayats were selected, two each from each district, where there are the maximum number of scheduled tribe population. A stratified random sampling technique had been employed for the selection of respondents for the purpose of detailed investigation. A pre-structured and pre-tested question schedule was employed for field survey (for sample questionnaire see appendix). But at the same time considering the peculiar historical background and ethical composition of the tribals who are living in forests, unstructured interviews were also conducted for qualitative data collection, especially to elicit information on socio-political aspects.

The survey has been conducted among eight tribal sections spread over eight panchayats in four districts of Kerala. The surveyed Panchayats include Peringamala and Vithura in Thiruvanathapuram district; Kulathupuzha and Themmala in Kollam district; Agali and Padur in Palakkad district and Mananthavadi and Panamaram in Wayanad district. The researcher included the major tribal groups of Kerala such as Paniyans, Kurichchans, Adiyans, Irulars, Mudugars, Kurumbas, Kanikars and Malai Pandarams as respondents. The details of the respondents are shown in Table 1.

The primary data was elucidated from the selected 400 tribals who are above the age of eighteen years - 100 from each district. The researcher has included political leaders, elected representatives, contested candidates in elections and those who are active in the socio-political organizations of tribals as respondents for his survey. They constitute about 20 percent of the respondents. A separate interview schedule was prepared for them and additional information was collected from this category and this forms the second part of this chapter (for sample questionnaire see appendix).

The field work was mainly carried out during the months of April and May 2006 and November and December 2006. For the analysis of the data, simple statistical tools were applied. Even though only 400 samples have been analaysed here, the researcher acquired a lot of information through discussing the problems with a host of others, who included Tribal Development Officials, Tribal Extension Officers, Tribal Promoters, socio-political activists belonging to tribal and non tribal sections, health officials, panchayat officials and so on. The information gathered from those sources provided much help to the researcher to generate a clear picture of the socialization and politicization process of the tribal community in Kerala.

Part I

Out of the 400 respondents, 162 were Kanikars (96 males and 66 females) and 38 were Malai pandarams (20 males and 18 females) who were selected from the four Panchayats of Thiruvananthapuram and Kollam districts. 30 Kurumbas (18 males and 12 females), 36 Irulars (23 males and 13 females) and 34 Mudugars (20 males and 14 females) were selected from the two panchayats of Palakkad district. 39 Paniyans (24 males and 15 females), 32 Kurichchans (21 males and 11 females) and 29 Adiyans (18 males and 11 females) were selected from Wayanad district.

On the basis of annual income the respondents are categorized into four groups as shown in Table 2. Since they have no permanent income, the income status of the respondents was decided on the basis of a rough calculation by the researcher and the respondents. It is

Table 1

Caste	*Male*	*Female*	*Total*
Kanikkar (Thiruvananthapuram District)	58	42	100
Malai Pandaram	20	18	38
Kanikkar (Kollam District)	38	24	62
Kurumbas	18	12	30
Irular	23	13	36
Mudugar	20	14	34
Paniyan	24	15	39
Kurichchan	21	11	32
Adiyan	18	11	29
Total	240	160	400

only a vauge calculation and not based on any authentic evidence. 31 percent of them have an annual income below Rs.3000. 37 percent belongs to an annual income group between 3001 and 5000. 17.5 percent belongs to the third group i.e., 5001-10,000 and the fourth group

Table 2
Annual Income (individual based)

Income of respondent	*No. of respondents*	*Percentage*
Below 3000	123	31
3001-5000	148	37
5001-10,000	71	17.5
Above 10,000	58	14.5

composed of 14.5 percent of the people with an annual income of Rs.10,000 and above. From the survey it is understood that economically the Kurichchyas are relatively well settled and the Adiyans and Paniyans remain underdeveloped even today.

As far as the educational status of the respondents are concerned, it is noted that 24.5 percent of them are illiterates and 48 percent of them are educated upto the school level. But only 15.5 percent of them completed the SSLC and 7 percent has completed the plus two course. 4.75 percent of them have degree or technical education. The researcher has been told that there are people who have medical and engineering degrees and are working in that capacity. Also the researcher got the information that students in all the four districts though a few in number are doing medical, engineering and post graduate studies. In my study Kurichchans and Kurumbas students are ranking first in education and they show more interest in sending their children to schools and colleges. Malai Pandarams and Paniyans shows very low interest in sending their children to schools. (see Table 3)

When the occupational status of the respondents are analysed, it is found that 52 percent of the respondents are employed as labourers. Most of them are agricultural labourers and others are working as casual labourers. A good number of them are also involved with the collection of Non Timber Forest Produces (NTFP). The respondents said that due to a number of reasons including the nationalization of some of the forest products and the reduced quantity of forest resources, they now no more concentrate in the

Table 3
Educational Qualification

Illiterate	*Below SSLC*	*SSLC*	*Plus 2, ITI etc*	*Degree or above or technical*
98	193	62	28	19
24.5%	48%	15.5%	7%	4.75%

collection of forest products as a livelihood, as it was in the past. In the case of Wayanad and Palakkad they get low payment for their work. The Paniyans belong chiefly to the labour class, but they do not get much work due to the fact that their labour is considered secondary. 22.75 percent of them are small scale farmers and 12 percent are employed in plantations and other private concerns. 4.5 percent of the respondents are government employees but working in lower grades and 8.75 percent are not engaged in any occupation due to physical incapability.

From the study the researcher clearly understood that land alienation is the chief issue of the tribals in Northern Kerala, especially in Wayanad and Palakkad.

Table 4
Occupational Status

Labour & NTFP collection	*Farmers*	*Private sector employment*	*Govt. servant*	*Unemployed*
208	91	48	18	35
52%	22.75%	12%	4.5%	8.75%

As shown in Table 5, the tribals lack landed property. 15.25% tribals are landless. Their condition is deplorable, especially in the case of Paniyans. 9.75 percent of the respondents possess land below 10 cents only. 28.75 percent have 11-50 cents of land and 22.25 percent possess 51 cents to 1 acre of land. 24 percent of the respondents possess more than one acre of land. The respondents of Wayanad and Palakkad blamed the settlers for making them landless. They told a number of incidents in which both avert and covert means have been applied by the settlers to snatch tribal land. While the more scrupulous persons acquired tribal land through cash purchase, the less scrupulous ones resorted to all sorts of practices to take possession of the tribal lands. A notable observation is that more than half of the land of the households in Wayanadu and Palakkadu have been alienated due to the influx of settlers.

It is also pointed out that in all the districts the landed tribals were mortgaging their land for raising money for ceremonies linked with marriage, birth and death, treatment of illness and for similar purposes. Loans were advanced in this way and when they failed to repay the debt along with interest, the land was legally transferred to the creditor. Another practice followed by the tribal land owners is that they would give out their land on lease to the migrant agriculturalists. Sobha kumari, the tribal panchayat member of Kulathupuzha panchayat, elected from Women (General) ward commented during an interview with the researcher that the practice of leasing of land is one of the chief reasons leading to the economic disempowerment of the tribals.

Table 5
Land Ownership

Landless	*Upto 10 cents*	*11-50 cents*	*51 –1 acre*	*More than 1 acre*
61	39	115	89	96
15.25%	9.75%	28.75%	22.25%	24%

In the survey respondents were selected only from among those who have completed eighteen years of age. 33 percent of the respondents came under the age group of 18-30 years. 31.5 percent belong to the age group of 31-40, 24.5 percent belongs to 41-60 age group and the remaining 11 percent are above 60 years of age (see Table 6).

Table 6
Age Group

18-30	*31-40*	*41-60*	*Above 60*
132	126	98	44
33%	31.5%	24.5%	11%

Generally the tribal sections of Kerala are interested in politics. Most of them are associating themselves with party politics. Almost all the political parties are functioning in tribal areas. Even there are followers of Kerala Congress which is known for its close relationship with settlers. The lone scheduled tribe reservation panchayat member in Kollam district A.S. Swapna is representing Kerala Congress (Joseph). In the survey 53 percent of the respondents expressed their open interest in politics (see the Table 7). But at the same time female respondents have shown comparatively lesser interest in politics. Majority of them expressed their belief that politicians have unholy nexuses with those who are disturbing them, which include liquor, forest and Ganja mafias.

Table 7

Interest in Politics	*No. of Respondents*	*Percent*
Yes	212	53
No	188	47

Out of the 53 percent who have interest in politics, 44.5% of people are participating in party activities like party meetings, committees, processions etc. It is also reported that the same people participate in the programmes of several parties. A number of people are attending meetings, processions etc. mainly due to their interest for a particular leader rather than their party interest.

52 percent of the respondents are open supporters of political parties and 48 percent are not openly supporting any political party as shown in Table 9. Even majority of the party supporters were not ready to reveal in which political party they belong to. But at

Table 8

Participation in party programmes	*No. of Respondents*	*Percent*
Yes	178	44.5
No	34	8.5

Table 9

Supports political parties	*No. of Respondents*	*Percent*
Yes	208	52
No	192	48

the same time it must be noted that left wing parties were very powerful in the past. But now their support base is declining.

The survey also shows that the tribals in Kerala are not a permanent vote bank of any political party. They are also in a position to evaluate the contribution of political parties for their cause. Only 42 percent of the respondents admitted that they are permanently voting to a political party without any change. But at the same time majority of the respondents are not the vote bank of any particular political party (Table 10). It shows the political attitude of the tribal people of Kerala.

Table 10

Permanent voter of a party	*No. of Respondents*	*Percent*
Yes	168	42
No	232	58

The fact that the respondents are interested in casting votes also shows their higher level of political and democratic awareness. 92 percent of the respondents said that they are casting votes in elections. Only 8 percent of people are not casting votes in elections (see Table 11). And out of these 8 percent, 6 percent of the people are not doing so deliberately. Only 8 respondents out of 400 are deliberately not casting votes in elections (see Table 12). It is mainly due to their personal grudge towards some political leaders.

Table 11

Casting votes in elections	*No. of Respondents*	*Percent*
Yes	368	92
No	32	8

Table 12

Deliberately not casting votes	*No. of Respondents*	*Percent*
Yes	8	2
No	24	6

The respondents made it clear that they are paying much attention to political campaigns. According to the survey, 87 percent of the respondents patiently listen to what the political parties and its leaders say. Only 13 percent have no interest in political campaigns (see Table 13). It is also noted by the respondents that, irrespective of political parties, the leaders are highlighting tribal issues at almost all the campaigns. They have also witnessed attractive offerings made during these campaigns. Some of them said that countless schemes were announced during the campaigns. But these schemes were never fully executed.

Table 13

Listening political campaigns	*No. of Respondents*	*Percent*
Yes	348	87
No	52	13

In general, majority of the tribals who participated in the survey believe that political parties are helpful to the development of their community. Some of them went to the extent of saying that political parties are indispensable for tribal development. Some describe political parties as the single largest agency which socialize and empower them politically. In the survey, 53 percent describe political parties as helpful and 42 percent have no such belief. 5 percent of the respondents especially women, are doubtful of the role of the political parties and they expressed no opinion on it (see Table 14).

Table 14

Opinion about political parties	*No. of Respondents*	*Percent*
Helpful	212	53
Not helpful	168	42
No opinion	20	5

The survey reveals that though the age of the urumoopan is over, they have respect and obedience to their tribal chief. Although he has no power and authority presently, they still respect him as in the past. The old generation have much respect for him where as

Table 15

Preference of government	*No. of Respondents*	*Percent*
Old tribal system	186	46.5
Modern system	214	53.5

the youngsters are not paying much respect to him. Now most of the urumoopans have clear party politics. A number of leaders and tribal panchayat representatives say that irrespective of party identity, they are obeying and respecting him. In the urusabha also, they are playing a major role. Even at present urumoopans play their role in resolving the conflicts among tribal people. Relating to the question of their preference of government, 46.5 percent supported the old tribal system where as the majority of them preferred modern democratic system of government (see Table 15). At the same time, 86.75 percent respondents made it clear that they are obeying and respecting their tribal chief (see Table 16). But at the same time not many of them are influenced by the chief in casting votes during elections. In the survey 59.25 percent belongs to this category (see Table 17). Thus we find that politicization of the tribal people of Kerala are progressing in a positive manner. Another interesting fact is that even those who are

Table 16

Respecting the tribal chief	*No. of Respondents*	*Percent*
Yes	347	86.75
No	53	13.25

Table 17

Influenced by tribal chief in casting votes	*No. of Respondents*	*Percent*
Yes	163	40.75
No	237	59.25

interested in party politics are showing respect to their tribal chiefs (see Table 18). The researcher's own analysis shows that the tribals in Kerala give high respect to their traditional culture and ways of living.

Table 18

Leader of choice	*No. of Respondents*	*Percent*
Tribal chief	328	82
Political leader	72	18

23 percent of the informants have direct link with political parties. Out of this 23 percent, 15.75 percent are members of various political parties while 7.25 percent are office holders as is shown in Table 19. A noticeable fact is that they are not getting adequate

Table 19

Relationship with political party	*No. of Respondents*	*Percent*
Member	63	15.75
Office holder	29	7.25
Neither	337	84.25

representation in political partys' high offices. On enquiry, a number of leaders said that tribals do not show much interest in taking such responsible posts. Laziness is inherent in a good majority of them. Competitive spirit is low among the tribals.

Many share the opinion that the political parties and candidates are giving presents in various forms to the tribals to canvas votes. But the survey report proves it more or less untrue. 16.75 percent of the respondents partially admitted it. The truth is that almost all of them get some liquor on the day before the election date. Some of them said that in the past, money was also distributed to the people. But now there is no such practice. 83.25 percent has not received any such presents for casting votes for a particular candidate (see Table 20). It shows that it is difficult to purchase the votes of tribals because they are democratically mature.

Table 20

Getting presents for votes	*No. of Respondents*	*Percent*
Yes	67	16.75
No	333	83.25

Another data which shows the political consciousness of tribal people is that 40 percent of them cast their votes after considering both the party and the personality of the candidate and 44.25 percent takes into account the party label of the candidate alone (see Table 21). It shows that the voting behaviour of the tribals of Kerala is in more or less the same pattern as that of the main land.

Table 21

Influential factor in voting	*No. of Respondents*	*Percent*
Party of the candidate	177	44.25
Personality	63	15.75
Both	160	40

In the traditional governance system of the tribals, there was male domination. But when the democratic system of government was established, females were also recruited to the ruling cadre. It is a truth that women are active in politics only due to the pressure of necessity. They have lesser interest to be in politics. 29.25 percent of the respondents admitted that there is male domination at the leadership level. But there is no hue and cry to change the situation. 70.75 percent of the respondents do not believe that there is male domination at the leadership levels (see Table 22).

Table 22

Opinion about male domination	*No. of Respondents*	*Percent*
Yes	117	29.25
No	283	70.75

Not even a single respondent from the districts of Kollam and Thiruvananthapuram states that there is enslavement from the settlers. But 7.25 percent of the respondents, those from Palakkad and Waynad, reported experience of enslavement, at least psychologically. Even though enslavement is abolished by law, it is heard

Table 23

Experience of enslavement	*No. of Respondents*	*Percent*
Yes	29	7.25
No	371	92.75

that it prevails in the tribal settlements, especially of Wayanad. But none of the respondents had experienced any direct enslavement.

The survey reveals the fact that a good majority of the tribals do not believe that the tribal leaders are powerful enough to protect them from the atrocities of settlers and the corrupt practice of government officials. 69.75 percent of the respondents believe so. (see Table 24). Some leaders from among them expressed the view that their protection is in their own hands and that such a feeling should be developed in their minds. At the same time, some of the respondents alleged that their leaders have some unholy nexus with the settlers and corrupted officials. Any way it is a fact that they could not be protected by a few leaders alone.

Table 24

Capability of tribal leaders to protect the tribals	*No. of Respondents*	*Percent*
Yes	121	30.25
No	279	69.75

79.25 percent of the respondents admitted that the tribal leaders including the elected representatives of

Pancyahati Raj Institutions are facing difficulties in opposing the settlers (see Table 5). According to them, the settlers have enough money and influence over the top leadership of all political parties. The local units of all parties are also availing themselves of financial help from the settlers. During times of election also the candidates including tribals are availing themselves of help from the settlers. A political leader from Wayanad observed that while the tribals are elected to Panchayat institutions, some of the settlers are elected as MLAs and MPS and could influence top political offices. They have direct link at the ministry level and with the top civil servants who draft policies. The coalition politics of Kerala provides good scope for the settlers.

Table 25

Difficult for the tribal leaders to oppose the settlers	*No. of Respondents*	*Percent*
Yes	317	79.25
No	83	20.75

A big majority of the respondents i.e., 83.25 percent, do not think that the present system of Panchayati Raj Institutions will shatter the traditional system of tribal governance (see Table 26). They think that the decline of tribal governance was due to a number of other reasons. One Panchayat member said that due to the decline of joint family system, when the members became economically independent and tried to live in their own way, the powers of uru governance and that of the mooppan began to decrease. Some others admitted that

Table 26

PRI will shatter the tribal governance system	*No. of Respondents*	*Percent*
Yes	67	16.75
No	333	83.25

the present urukootam will definitely fill the vaccum created as a result of the decline of their traditional uru sabha functioned in each settlement and acted with full authority on all matters related to the uru.

A good majority of the respondents i.e., 76.75 percent, believe that the new Panchayati Raj Institutions will empower the tribal sections. Some of the respondents have the opinion that the PRIs should be empowered enough to regain the tribals their old rights, including the right to manage natural resources such as land, water, forest etc. But at the same time, 23.35 percent of the respondents do not believe so (see Table 27). Some of them believe that the inauguration of the new PRIs resulted in the weakening of their traditional system of informal government.

Table 27

PRI will empower the tribal sections	*No. of Respondents*	*Percent*
Yes	307	76.75
No	93	23.25

The majority of the respondents are of the opinion that they are participating in the urukuttom with great

Table 28

Participation in democratic process	*No. of Respondents*	*Percent*
Urukuttom alone	280	70
Grama Sabha alone	Nil	-
Neither	63	15.75
Both	57	14.25

interest. The urukuttam is held regularly before the meeting of the Grama Sabha of the ward. But the survey shows that they are participating more in the urukuttom than in the Grama Sabha. The records also prove this true. When 70 percent of the respondents are participating in the urukuttom, only 14.25 percent of them are attending the Grama Sabha (see the Table 28). An interesting fact is that not even a single respondent said that he is attending the Grama Sabha alone. It is also seen that women respondents are very eager to attend the urukootam. It is also found in the records of majority of the urukuttoms.

Relating to the organization and functioning of urukuttom, most respondents are not at all satisfied. Only 22.25 percent of the respondents expressed full satisfaction in its functioning while 29 percent are satisfied to a certain extent. But 48.75 percent of them are not at all satisfied with the functioning of urukuttom (See Table 29). The chief complaint is that some vested interests are subverting the actual priority while selecting the beneficiaries.

Table 29

Satisfaction in the functioning of urukuttom	*No. of Respondents*	*Percent*
Satisfied	89	22.25
Not satisfied	195	48.75
To a certain extent	116	29

A good majority of the respondents are of the opinion that they are presenting their issues in urukuttom but seldom in Grama Sabha. Only 19.75 percent do not have such an opinion as shown in Table 30. Out of the 77.75 percent of the respondents, who are making presentations in urukuttom, 42.75 are satisfied and believe that their opinions get adequate attention there. But 35 percent made the complaint that their opinions are not getting adequate attention in the urukuttom (See Table 31). Some of them have the opinion that unnecessary political interferences are there in the urukuttom.

Another interesting fact is that majority of them expressed dissatisfaction in the performance of their elected representatives. 51.75 percent of them have the

Table 30

Made presentations in Urukuttom / Grama Sabha	*No. of Respondents*	*Percent*
Yes	311	77.75
No	79	19.75

Table 31

Opinions get adequate attention	*No. of Respondents*	*Percent*
Yes	171	42.75
No	140	35

feeling that they have voted not to the right candidate (see Table 32). The reason behind such an opinion is that their representatives are promoting their private and party interests rather than the well being of the tribals.

Table 32

Voted to the right candidate	*No. of Respondents*	*Percent*
Yes	193	48.25
No	207	51.75

Half of the respondents are of the opinion that the tribal leaders and representatives are actually promoting tribal interests. But at the same time, an equal number of respondents are strongly opposing the view (see Table 33). They raised a number of allegations against their leaders. The first allegation is that they are getting financial and other supports from the settlers and other vested interests. It is also found that those who are supported by the settlers often get party tickets to contest elections. Some of the respondents are of the opinion that due to various pressures, the tribal leaders and representatives are closing their eye towards some burning issues of the tribals. Some of the elected representatives also expressed the opinion that they are forced to function by party direction. All these show that the tribal leaders and representatives have not became proportionately powerful and influential leaders as those in the general category.

Table 33

Leaders are promoting tribal interest	*No. of Respondents*	*Percent*
Yes	203	50.75
No	197	49.25

It is interesting that 54.25 percent of the respondents are optimistic of restoring their old power and property status through political empowerment. They are also of the opinion that the new PRIs are stepping stones in this direction. Some of them believe that the dream would be fulfilled only when one of their representative will be there at the secretariat as a minister. They expressed their hope that their dream would get fulfilled in near future.

Table 34

Believe in restoring their old status	*No. of Respondents*	*Percent*
Yes	217	54.25
No	183	45.75

The majority of the respondents are not at all optimistic of the scope for a tribal political organization outside the perview of the mainstream political parties in Kerala. 59.25 percent respondent share the opinion (see Table 35). They also think that they have a number of limitations to shape such organizations. Their backwardness and their low population are the primary factors that limit them. They argue that they can gain a lot if they go along with the mainstream political parties. Some of them have the view that in the coalition politics of the state, they have also a role to play. But at the same time, 40.75 percent see the scope of a political organization for the tribals outside the perview of the mainstream political parties in Kerala. But at the same time they are not fully optimistic of its realization chiefly because of the strong party politics prevailing in tribal areas. They also alleged that such a move would be prevented by the political parties, the settlers and the bureaucrats. But at the same time they believe that such a move alone can give maximum benefits to the tribals in Kerala.

Table 35

Scope for a tribal party	*No. of Respondents*	*Percent*
Yes	163	40.75
No	237	59.25

Part II

Out of the 400 respondents, 64 are playing some role in politics as party leaders, contestants in elections, elected representatives in Panchayati Raj Institutions etc. A separate interview schedule was distributed to them to collect additional information.

Out of these 64 respondents, 56 of them have clear party connections and are active in politics. The other 8 respondents made it clear that they are with the tribals and not with any political parties. Two among this eight are very critical of political parties. Both of them have contested in the last panchayat elections and lost. The 56 respondents who are active in political parties admitted that they are working with parties to protect the tribal interests. 28 of them also admitted that they were interested in the ideology and style of functioning of their parties.

Out of the 56 political functionaries, only 18 of them expressed satisfaction in the approach of their political party towards tribal issues. 12 respondents made it clear that parties have their own limits to do much for the benefit of such a small section of people. 26 of them went to the extent of saying that their political parties contributed much for the well being of the tribals.

36 respondents said that they would remain with the tribals, if their political party take a stand which is contradictory to the interests of the tribals. 11 respondents stated that political parties are functioning above sectarian interests and their party is not a tribal party. 9 of them are optimistic that their party will not take decisions that harm tribal interests.

48 respondents got different levels of training. They reported that the training was effective to enhance their leadership qualities. Out of the 56 political functionaries, 14 of them did not respond to the question of getting party posts and positions to tribal people But 26 respondents have made it clear that they have not

been denied any post in the party just because of their being a tribal. K. Murugan, a tribal leader belonging to Irular community and a member of the Attappady Block Panchayat in Palakkad District said that his party has always treated him fairly and he was given deserving responsibilities as a party member. He also noted that tribals do not come up to hold high party offices mainly because of their general character of laziness and lack of interest.

But 16 respondents alleged that political parties are showing discrimination towards tribals while selecting the leaders even at the lower strata of the parties. Sreelatha Sivanandan and Hari Kumar, the tribal members of Peringamala Grama Panchayat Committee in Thiruvananthapuram District have this opinion and added that the political parties of Kerala in general are consciously avoiding tribal people from responsible posts and positions even though they are deserving. (The two members belong to two prominent political parties). Eettimoodu Rajendran, the Secretary of Tribal Service Society, Thiruvananthapuram District stated that tribal empowerment would be possible only by uniting them outside the mainstream party politics.

Out of the 64 respondents, 38 of them contested in the last two panchayat elections. 36 of them have contested in the reservation seats. Only 24 of them won in these election and 19 of them are panchayat members at present.

All the 36 contestants admitted that they have contested as a result of the pressure from various quarters, including party and people. It is interesting that cent percent of them became a candidate in election because they were motivated by the leaders and the villagers. All of them also admitted that the decision to contest was not taken personally. Out of the 38 contested candidates, 36 of them had contested in reservation constituency. They also admitted that they contested only because reservation facility was made available, otherwise they may not have contested. Thampu, an S.T. member of the Panamaram Grama Panchayat in Waynad District who belongs to the Adiya Community said, "as far as me and my Adiya Community are concerned, the reservation facility alone helped us to contest and get elected to the panchayat governing committee". Reservation of seats in PRIs is highly beneficial to the tribal community especially to the Adiyas and Paniyas.

From the study it is clear that 80 percent of the contestants in the tribal areas have no idea about the application of any specific technique to win the elections. But in non tribal areas of Kerala, majority of the candidates arc applying special techniques to win elections. Out of the 24 elected persons, 19 of them believed that their sponsoring political parties are responsible for their victory. Most of them also admitted that their personal charisma also shares the cause of their victory.

Four of them admitted that caste is also a factor that influenced the victory of a candidate though not a prominent one.

Another interesting factor which makes elections in tribal area unique is that money has a limited role in the victory of candidates there. The usual practice is that the candidates are personally approaching the voters. All of them admitted that they approached each voter in person to assure votes. In this respect campaigning was very serious. 90 percent of the candidates said that the maximum amount they spent from their pocket was less than Rs.1000. At the same time many of the respondents indirectly pointed out the evil influence of alcohol and drugs. Sobha Kumari, a female tribal member from Kulathupuzha Panchayat in Kollam District and Sulochana, another female tribal member of Panamaram Grama Panchayat in Waynad District emphasized the negative impact of alcohol on tribal vote especially males. They added that the tribal community can be liberated only through imposing prohibition of liquor in its real sense. A good number of youth, who are the promises of tomorrow are addicted to this vice and must be rescued.

Almost all the respondents admitted that the reservation facility under the 73rd constitution amendment would definitely accelerate the political empowerment of the tribals. From the study, it is clear that the Panchayati Raj Act motivated the scheduled tribes towards political socialization and political participation, thereby empowering them politically. A large number of them are motivated to contest in elections, which increased the number of tribals who were recruited in politics. The elected people got an opportunity to share the administration of Panchayati Raj Institutions as representatives. It helped to evolve effective leadership from the tribal people in the state. But at the same time the research reveals the fact that majority of them, particularly at the lower level, are less educated, ignorant, inexperienced, poor, first generation entries and relatively less exposed to the outside world.

Most of the elected members admitted that during times of election, they had only limited knowledge of the functioning of Panchayati Raj system. They heard about Grama Sabha and the like through informal sources, i.e., local politicians, ex-panchayat members, other panchayat representatives etc. However after becoming panchayat members and after going through the training processes, many of them have enhanced their level of awareness about the functioning of Panchayat Raj Institutions. As an extension faculty member of the Kerala Institute of Local Administration (KILA) and from his own close association with tribals in the training programmes and training faculties of KILA, the researcher have experienced the behavioural changes and leadership qualities acquired by the tribal leaders, who are the representatives of various Panchayati Raj Institutions. From the talks the researcher had with the tribal representatives who had undergone training in KILA, he could find that they had acquired a lot regarding leadership techniques and they were going back to their destinations with definite future plans for the development of the common tribals. The tribal leader C. Santamony who is the President of Agali Grama Panchayat in Palakkad District stated that she underwent truing at KILA thrice, which undoubtedly improved her efficiency as the President of Grama Panchayat.

The adequate training facilities available in the state of Kerala provided them with material inputs and motivated them to take active part in the identification of the local level problems and their management. A number of tribal Panchayat members, who attended training suggested that orientation programmes should be conducted in regular intervals at block or district level. They admitted that the complicated procedures of the PRI, made it difficult for the representatives to function effectively. Such training alone makes the functioning of the system smooth and effective. K. Ammu, the female President of Mananthavadi Block Panchayat of Waynad District who belonged to the Kurichchya section of Scheduled Tribe, strongly argued for the necessity of compulsory training programmes at least for the newly elected members. K.M. Varky Master, the President of the Mananthavadi Grama Panchayat pointed out the need to extent training to the tribal masses at least at the ward level. They should be made aware of the role of urukuttom and Gramasabha in empowering them politically and socially.

During the interview, some of the members also suggested that the orientation programmes should be extended to the common tribal people at the panchayat level as a part of their political empowerment. In their opinion, such a training will definitely add to the meaning and strength of Grama Sabha and urukuttom. It is advisable that people and their representatives will take interest in Panchayat so that the voice of the poor tribals is properly heard by high level officials. Grama sabha meetings should be timely and successfully organized and the resolutions passed and forwarded by the apex body.

All the 24 elected members, admitted that they have tried their best to organize the urukuttom in an effective manner. But at the same time they admitted that most of the urukuttoms are not getting organized or functioning well. They admitted that the Grama Sabha is not effectively functioning due to the lack of meaningful participation of people in it. It is a truth that at a number of places, the Grama Sabha meetings are conducting with thin attendance and there was no serious debates and discussions taken place. Some of the respondents who are not elected representatives said that in some places, the representatives as well as the bureaucracy had not take much effort in strengthening urukuttoms. They alleged that the urukuttom meetings were organized in some places without adequate publicity. The Agali Grama Panchayat handbook on Tribal Subplan 2007-2008 states that the tribals are not now retaining their initial interest in urukuttom and Grama Sabhas as it was in the early stages of the New Panchayati Raj system. It was justified by Padmini Madhavan Kani, a female tribal member of the Vithura Grama Panchayat in Thiruvananthapuram District, who was also the Vice President of the Panchayat last time. She stated that funding was not adequate and the deserved hands for benefits are too many. This at times resulted in conflicts in the urukuttom while selecting the beneficiaries. She added that she still lived in a bamboo hut and could never avail herself of the opportunity to have funding for a better house. Another allegation is that the proceedings of grama sabha were written down even without the knowledge of those who attended it. But the allegation was strongly opposed by eighty percentage of the elected representatives who responded to the researcher.

All the 64 respondents believe that the planning and implementation of the tribal schemes from top to bottom in not in a transparent manner. They also wanted to make it more transparent by appointing tribal people, who are properly trained in this field, in proper places. For that purpose, it is suggested by some respondents that the PRIs in tribal areas should be given more powers and functions. Resources must flow to these institutions and its ever increasing powers and authority might generate some interest in the tribal people. This interest is likely to translate into reality a better participative leadership at the grass-root level. If the participation of the tribals in grass-root level institutions is ensured properly, their political recruitment will be made easy and thereby provide better socialization and politicization. Such developments will definitely better their educational, economic and other conditions and they would be easily lifted to the mainstream life of the nation.

The respondents also admitted that their opinions as well as that of other tribal leaders are getting due consideration in shaping the tribal policies at the party level. But at the same time some of the tribal leaders opened their heart saying that the tribal leaders and representatives have limited or no control over the source of power. They pointed out that the tribal representatives including the Presidents of Panchayats are dependent on the leaders belonging to the general strata. When the researcher raised the question 'can the tribal leaders do more justice to their tribal people?', some of the tribal representatives and leaders admitted that they act according to the decision taken by the party. One respondent pointed out that even the beneficiary lists are being prepared in party offices than in urukuttoms. But it was strongly opposed by majority of the Panchayat representatives.

Out of the total 64 respondents, 52 of them revealed that they are not fully satisfied with their performance as tribal leaders.

More than 90 percent of the respondents, supported the implementation of reservation of posts and position in political parties for tribals. Some of them pointed out the fact that the tribals have no representation in the upper strata leadership of almost all parties. The respondents also described it a necessity to get adequate opportunity to them to express their needs and wants at higher platforms of their party. It was also suggested that the leaders belonging to the general category should show much more concern in the affairs of the tribal people for their empowerment.

8

Conclusion

It is found during the course of the study that the process of political socialization and political participation were improved especially after the introduction of the New Panchayati Raj Institutions which gave more opportunities and power to the tribal community. The resurgence of tribal political institutions like Urukootams helped to improve the political socialization and political participation of tribal communities in a more meaningful manner. If the tribals are given much more participation in the governing process at least in the PRIs, it would better their political socialization and development.

Almost all the political parties in Kerala have their units in the tribal areas. Though the tribals were not given high posts in party offices, to some extent they are recruited as party office holders. The parties also give training and orientations to the tribal party members as well as the tribal masses. It is also observed that it was the political parties that had played a major role in the political socialization process of the tribal community in Kerala.

The vested interests of the immigrants and their influence on the decision makers are the major hindrance to the empowerment of the tribals. Often the tribals stand in the way of their own development by becoming instruments in the hands of vested interests. The addiction for alcohol found chiefly among tribal males, proves to be another major hindrance in the path of their political empowerment and development. Most of the tribal sects show a lack of concern for providing modern education to the youngsters. It had definitely affected in a negative manner, their political socialization, participation and empowerment.

Though the tribal ones tried to formulate their own political platforms outside the mainstream political parties and made some efforts to bring the entire tribal sects under its umbrella to fight against tribal injustice, it didn't work as they intended. At present, the tribals do not consider it practical to have a political base outside the mainstream politics of Kerala.

Summary of the findings

1. The political empowerment of the tribals plays a crucial role in shaping the development strategies of their plans and schemes.

2. Proper political socialization and participation alone can ensure tribal empowerment.

3. The tribal community was once the masters of the tribal land, which constitute a big chunk of the state's forest area.

4. Conscious attempts to disempower the tribal sections began during the British period.

5. Independent India had a clear vision on tribal issues and accordingly shaped schemes and programmes for improving the process of political socialization and participation among the tribals.

6. The Indian Constitution too provided several provisions for the empowerment of the tribal masses of the country. The Constitution aimed at uplifting and bringing to the fore, the hither to backward sections of the society including the tribals. Since it was declared a national goal, the Kerala Government, following the footsteps of the Central and other state governments, took initiatives in launching several pro-tribal policies and created a wide network of developmental administration to bring about radical changes in the life of the tribal community in the state.

7. From the study it is clear that almost all the political parties in the state have their party units in tribal segments. They play a major role in socializing and politically participating the tribals of Kerala. Though the tribals were not proportionately given key posts and positions in the parties, they were recruited in party offices to some extent. During elections, the tribals mostly contested in the tickets of various political parties.

The tribal elected representatives were given proper orientations and trainings at party levels.

8. Owing to the peculiar political situation in Kerala, the Left Democratic Front and the United Democratic Front which alternatively is in office in the state, are always under the pressure of the settlers and other vested interests. It prevents the government as well as political parties from implementing constructive and strong programmes for the empowerment of the tribal sections. The tribal population of the state being small in size and that too scattered over various districts and also not a political force, cannot form a pressure group to make the government and political parties to get things done in their favour.

9. The new Panchayati Raj Institutions provided ample scope for improving the political participation of the tribals. The Urukuttom and Gramasabha offered them opportunities to formulate and implement schemes and programmes to meet their social needs, to mobilize them, to chanalize their energies towards socio-economic reconstruction and to involve them in the developmental programmes of their communities through their own forums. No doubt, it directly as well as indirectly accelerated the process of political socialization of the tribals more than ever.

10. The political socialization process helped them realize that they were not able to influence the rulers properly to get things done in their favour. They also identified the reason for this as that they

had not emerged as a pressure group in Kerala Politics or as a significant social group with economic power. As a result they began to think of shaping new strategies to protect themselves from social exclusion, political and economic disempowerment and various forms of exploitation.

11. As a part of the endeavour to formulate a new tribal policy, their issues especially related to land alienation were politicized by their leaders like C.K. Janu and Geethanandan. The issues were discussed in most of the tribal settlements in the state. It brought the process of political socialization of the tribals in Kerala to new heights. It is this newly born awareness about their problems and conditions, that become the leading spirit behind the 47 days tribal agitation beside Government Secretariat, Thiruvananthapuram in 2001 and the Muthanga agitation in Wayanad in January 2003. Subsequently new tribal forums like the Adivasi-Dalit Samara Samiti, the Adivasi Gothra Mahasabha and the Rashritiya Mahasabha were launched outside the mainstream politics of the state. However, since the tribals constitute only 1.4 percent of the total population of the state, their own separate organizations and movements proved inefficient to empower them.

12. From the study, the researcher observed that land alienation and exploitation of their ignorance and innocence were the chief reasons behind the disempowerment of the tribals of Kerala. Acute poverty, negation of rights, exploitation by

intermediaries, lack of proper education, lack of employment opportunities, laziness and addiction to alcohol were the other reasons for their disempowerment. Better socialization and orientation alone could liberate the tribal sections from their present state.

13. Now the tribals in Kerala show more interest in mainstream political parties rather than their own forums. A good number of them are politically conscious and are attending political party programmes and they constitute a mass base to most of the political parties in tribal areas. But at the same time they are not the vote bank of a particular political party. They are keenly observing the policies of parties and are responding with vigour. They have respect towards their traditional political system and at the same time no hesitation to join hands with the modern participatory democracy.

14. Their voting pattern and behaviour also shows that they have attained political maturity. Their increased participation in Urukuttoms and Gramasabha also shows their political awareness and participatory spirit.

15. The members and leaders of various political parties recruited from among the tribals have also proved to be effective. They were given trainings by the parties concerned. The representatives of PRIs are also trained well in institutions like KILA and KIRTHADS. The researcher has experienced the positive behavioural changes and leadership qualities acquired by them.

The tribal settlements have experienced numerous developmental activities and the development agencies have been pumping in huge funds into the tribal areas for their all round development. The government has also giant schemes for the purpose. But the yard sticks of development prepared by those staying in the well equipped offices are insufficient to measure the needs and wants of the tribal people. Tribal development in the real sense can be achieved only through planning and implementing schemes and programmes with the co-operation and participation of the tribals. The tribal empowerment could be fulfilled only by ensuring their socialization and participation. So in place of large schemes and huge funding, simple measures should be adopted from the lower levels to make them aware of their needs. They should be allowed to decide the shape of their own lives through their own programmes implemented through them. The required amount of resources, personnel and other facilities should be dripped to them whenever and wherever needed. The researcher hopes that the study would direct the attention of the planners and administrators towards creating a self sufficient and sustainable tribal society, were the tribals have an voice in determining and implementing strategies for their growth and development. The message of the study is that the development strategy for a society should be formulated only after knowing the heart beats of the society.

Appendix

Table 1
Scheduled Tribes of Kerala

Sl. No.	*Tribe*	*Location (District)*
1	Adiyan	Wayanad
2	Arandan	Malappuram
3	Eravallan	Palakkad
4	Hill Pulaya	Idukki
5	Irular / Irulan	Palakkad
6	Kadar	Palakkad, Thrissur
7	Kammara	—
8	Kanikkar / Kanikaran	Thiruvananthapuram, Kollam
9	Karimbalan	—
10	Kattunayakan	Wayanad, Malappuram
11	Kochuvelan	Pathanamthitta
12	Kondakapus	—
13	Kondareddis	—

(Contd.)

(Contd. Table 1)

Sl. No.	*Tribe*	*Location (District)*
14	Koraga	Kasaragod
15	Kota	Wayanad
16	Kudiya, Melakudi	Kasaragod
17	Kurichchan	Wayanad, Kozhikode & Kannur
18	Kurumans	Wayanad
19	Kurumbas	Palakkad
20	Maha Malasar	Palakkad
21	Malai Arayan	Idukki, Kottayam
22	Malai Pandaram	Kollam, Pathanamthitta
23	Malai Vedan	Kollam, Pathanamthitta
24	Malakkuravan	Kollam, Pathanamthitta
25	Malasar	Palakkad
26	Malayan	Thrissur, Ernakulam
27	Malayarayar	Idukki, Kottayam
28	Mannan	Idukki
29	Mavilan	
30	Muthuvan/Mudugar / Muduvan	Palakkad / Idukki
31	Palleyan	Idukki
32	Palliyan	Idukki
33	Palliyar	Idukki
34	Paniyan	Wayanad, Kozhikodu, Kannur, Malappuram
35	Ulladan	Kollam, Alapuzha, Ernakulam, Pathanamthita,

(Contd.)

(Contd. Table 1)

Sl. No.	*Tribe*	*Location (District)*
		Kottayam, Idukki, Thrissur
36	Uraly	Idukki

Kammara is a Telugu speaking community not found commonly in Kerala, but some members are found here and there.

Kondakapus – This Telugu speaking community is in A.P. and not seen in Kerala

Kondareddis – Same as Kondakapus

Source : Scheduled Tribes of Kerala at a Glance, KIRTADS, Kozhikode.

Table 2

Scheduled tribe population in Kerala (2001)

Sl.No.	*District*	*District wise*				
		Male	*Female*	*Total*	*Percent*	*Percent of the total population*
1.	Kasaragod	15132	15206	30338	8.33	2.52
2.	Kannur	9793	10176	19969	5.48	0.82
3.	Wayanad	67394	68668	136062	37.36	17.43
4.	Kozhikode	2924	3016	5940	1.63	0.21
5.	Malappuram	5996	6271	12267	3.36	0.34
6.	Palakkad	19990	19675	39665	10.89	1.52
7.	Thrissur	2293	2533	4826	1.33	0.16

(Contd.)

(Contd. Table 2)

Sl.No.	*District*	*District wise*			*Percent*	*Percent of the total population*
		Male	*Female*	*Total*		
8.	Ernakulam	5079	4967	10046	2.76	0.32
9.	Idukki	25510	25463	50973	14.00	4.51
10.	Kottayam	8972	9368	18340	5.04	0.94
11.	Alappuzha	1565	1566	3131	0.86	0.15
12.	Pathanamthitta	3184	3365	6549	1.8	0.53
13.	Kollam	2447	2743	5190	1.43	0.20
14.	Thiruvananthapuram	9890	11003	20893	5.74	0.65
	Total	180169	184020	364189	100.00	1.14

Source: Government of Kerala, 2006: Economic Review, State Planning Board, Thiruvananthapuram

Table 3
Landless Tribal Families – District Wise

Sl.No.	*District*	*Landless Families*	*Land below 1 acre*
1.	Thiruvananthapuram	13	1101
2.	Kollam	10	572
3.	Pathanamthitta	54	1032
4.	Alappuzha	3	568
5.	Kottayam	134	1340
6.	Idukki	-	4458
7.	Ernakulam	-	724
8.	Thrissur	251	840

(Contd.)

(Contd. Table 3)

Sl.No.	*District*	*Landless Families*	*Land below 1 acre*
9.	Palakkad	5379	2637
10.	Malappuram	178	2224
11.	Kozhikode	0	787
12.	Wayanad	12564	12184
13.	Kannur	655	2249
14.	Kasaragod	157	171
	Total	19398	30887

Source: Government of Kerala, 2006 Economic Review, State Planning Board, Thiruvananthapuram

Table 4

Deprivation status of basic amenities like house, drinking water, latrin, electricity connection of Scheduled Tribes in Kerala

Sl.No.	*District*	*Society in General*	*Rank*	*Scheduled Tribe*	*Rank*
1.	Thiruvananthapuram	39.5	11	60.1	10
2.	Kollam	30.4	8	50.7	5
3.	Pathanamthitta	31.1	9	54.6	7
4.	Alappuzha	29.6	6	40.1	3
5.	Kottayam	25.1	3	43.1	4
6.	Idukki	42.7	13	65.3	13
7.	Ernakulam	15.5	1	37.2	1
8.	Thrissur	24.7	2	37.5	2

(Contd.)

(Contd. Table 4)

Sl.No.	District	Society in General	Rank	Scheduled Tribe	Rank
9.	Palakkad	40.4	12	65.3	12
10.	Malappuram	28.6	5	56.8	8
11.	Kozhikode	28.3	4	50.9	6
12.	Wayanad	46.3	14	66.00	14
13.	Kannur	29.7	7	57.7	9
14.	Kasaragod	37.6	10	61.3	11
	State Average	29.5		57.9	

Source: Government of Kerala, 2006: Economic Review, State Planning Board, Thiruvananthapuram.

Table 5
Tribal Land Alienation for Dams

Project	*Area (hectares)*
Parampikkulam-Aaliyar	2389.665
Mullapperiyar	2890.000
Bhuthathankettu	608.00
Valayar	259.000
Peechi	1263.000
Vazhani	255.000
Neryamangalam	413.000
Kundala	230.000
Aanayirangal	433.000
Ponmudi	260.000
Poringalkkuthu	263.000
Chenkulam	33.000
Others	16627.650
Total	25924.315

Source: P.K. Prakash, 2002, *Anyadheenappedunna Bhoomi – Adivasi Bhoomi Presnathinte Charithravum Rashtriyavum* (Mal.) Kozhikode – 2, p. 70.

Table 6
Land Alienation for Wildlife Sanctuaries

Name	*Area (Square km)*
Periyar Wild Life Sanctuary	77.00
Neyyar	128.00
Peechi Vazhani	125.00
Parampikulam	285.00

(Contd.)

(Contd. Table 6)

Name	*Area (Square km)*
Wayanad	344.44
Idukki	70.00
Peppara	53.00
Chimmini	85.00
Chinnar	90.44
Sentharunni	100.32
Aarallam	55.00
Thattekkad Bird Sanctuary	25.00
Eravikulam National Park	97.00
Silent Valley	84.52
Nilgiri Biosphere	1455.00
Agasthyavanam Biological Park	23.00
Total Conservation Area	2324.72

Source: P.K. Prakash (2002), p. 69.

Table 7
Forest Lands Appropriated for Non-Forest Purpose

Sl.No.	*Purpose*	*Area (Hectare)*
1.	Kerala Plantation Corporation	11704.754
2.	Oil Palm India	3645.640
3.	Punalur Rehabilitation Plantation	2265.218
4.	State Farming Corporation	2467.040
5.	Various Hydro-electric projects	14169.650
6.	Irrigation Projects	6475.000
7.	Arable Land	8074.230
8.	Tropical Botanical Garden	121.340
9.	Valayal Malabar Cements	328.65

(Contd.)

(Contd. Table 7)

Sl.No.	*Purpose*	*Area (Hectare)*
10.	Kerala Wood Industries, Nilampoor	17.640
11.	Rubber Board	299.019
12.	U.S.S.C	115.400
13.	Mattupetti Indo-Swiss Project	39.150
14.	Trivandrum Mineral Water	32.000
15.	KFRI, Peechi	28.174
16.	CPCRI, Kasargode	121.960
17.	Coffee Board	116.24
18.	Water Distribution Projects	582.000
19.	Electric Lines	597.785
20.	Settlements	17100.000
21.	Encroachment in Cardamom Hill Reserve	81400.000
22.	In various Forest Divisions	18600.000
23.	Mullapperiyar Project in Thekkadi	2890.000
24.	Parampikkulam Aaliyar Project	2384.665
25.	For Lease in Various Divisions	8734.105
	Total	182618.66

Source: P.K. Prakash (2002), p. 73.

Bibliography

Primary Source

Constitution of AGMS, published by AGMs

Constitution of India

Government of India : Census of India 1991

Government of India : Census of India 2001

Government of India : The Scheduled Tribe and Other Traditional Forest Dwellers (Recognition of Forest Rights) Act 2006, The Gazette of India 2007.

Govt. of Kerala, Scheduled Caste and Scheduled Tribe Colonies, Website: kerala.gov.org. july 28, 2003.

Govt. of Kerala : Administrative Report 2001, Department of Revenue.

Govt. of Kerala : Kerala Gazette (Extra Ordinary) dated 14-11-1975, Notification No. 673, Trivandrum.

Govt. of Kerala : Kerala Gazette (Extra Ordinary) dated 20-10-86, Notification No. 934, Trivandrum.

Govt. of Kerala : Scheduled Tribes Development Programmes – 2006-07, Dept. of Tribal Development.

Govt. of Kerala : Scheduled Tribes of Kerala at a Glance – 2003, KIRTADS, Kozhikode.

Govt. of Kerala : Notification No. M.S. 575/64/A.D dated 19-8-1964, Trivandrum.

Govt. of Kerala : Notification No. 22363/leg.A1/98/Law dated 9-3-1999, Trivandrum.

Govt. of Kerala : Socio-Economic Survey of Tribal Communities – 1989, Dept. of Tribal Development.

Govt. of Kerala : Tribal Mission Report – 2002, Dept. of Tribal Development.

Govt. of Travancore : 1948, Acts and Proclamations of Travancore, Trivandrum.

High Court of Kerala : Judgement KLT 1069/1970/HCK, Ernakulam.

The Kerala Legislative Assembly : Bill No. 160, dated 23-9-1996, Trivandrum.

Secondary Source

(a) Books

Almond, Gabriel and James S. Coleman (eds) *Politics of Developing Areas,* New Jersey, Princeton University Press, 1960.

Alcof, Linda Martin, *Philosophy and Racial Identity*, Temple University Press, 1997.

Alexander, K.C., R.R. Prasad, M.P. Jahangirdar, *Tribals: Rehabilitation and Development*, Jaipur, Rawat Publications, 1991.

Bhaskaran, *'Janu' Biography*, Kottayam, D.C. Books, 2003.

Boban K. Jose, *Tribal Ethnomedicine: Continuity and Change*, New Delhi : APH Publishing Corporation, 1998.

Burman, Roy, B.K., *Challenges and Response in Tribal India*, M.S.A. Rao (ed), Social Movements in India, New Delhi, 1979.

Chathukulam, Jose and M.S. John, "Issues in Tribal Development, The Recent Experience of Kerala", in Govinda Chandra Rath (ed.) *Tribal Development in India : The Contemporary Debate*, New Delhi, Sage Publications India Pvt. Ltd., 2006.

Chathukulam, Jos, C.V. Balamurali and K.M. Jayan, *Study on Special Component Plan and Tribal Subplan under Decentralized Planning Process in Kerala*, Kottayam, Centre for Rural Management, 2000.

Chaudhuri, Budhadeo (ed.), *Tribal Development in India*, New Delhi: Inter India Publications, 1982.

Das, Pravakar, *Emerging Pattern of Leadership in Tribal India*, New Delhi, Manak Publications Pvt. Ltd., 1994.

Dowse, Robert and John Hughes, *Political Socialization*, London, Princeton University Press, 1972.

Dube, S.C. (ed.), *Tribal Heritage of India,* New Delhi, Vikas Publishing House, 1977.

Gandhi, M.K., *Village Swaraj* (Completed by H.M. Vyas) Ahemadabad, Navjeevan Publishing House, 1953.

Ghate, Ruchas, *Forest Policy and Tribal Development,* New Delhi: Concept Publishing Company, 1992.

Ghosh, P.K., *Tribals and Their Culture – Manipur and Nagaland,* Vol. 3, New Delhi, Ashish Publishing House, 1992.

Ghosh, Ratna, and Alok Kumar Pramanik (ed), *Panchayat System in India : Historical Constitutional and Financial Analysis,* New Delhi, Kanishka Publishers, 1999.

Ghurye, G.S., *The Aborigines So-called and Their Future,* Poona, Gokhale Institute of Politics and Economics, 1943.

Issac, Thomas, *Local Democracy and Development,* New Delhi, Leftward Publishers, 2000.

Janu, C.K. and M. Geethanandan, *Adivasi Grama Panchayathum Swayambharanavum* (Mal.), Cochin, Clan n' Culture, 2001.

Janu, C.K., M. Geethanandan, *Muthangayilekkulla Thiruchupokku – Oru Sathyavangmoolam,* Published by AGMS, 2003.

Johari, J.C., *Comparative Politics,* New Delhi, Sterling Publishers Pvt. Ltd., 1992.

Johnson Vadakumchery, *Tribes and Cultural Ecology in General India*, New Delhi, Mittal Publications, 2003.

Kattakayam, Jacob John, *Social Structure and Change Among the Tribals*, Delhi, B.R. Publishing Corporation, II ed., 2001.

Karunakaran C.K, *Aadivasikalude Lokam: Vtanavasikal* (Mal.) Thiruvananthapuram, Kerala Bhasha Institute, 2007.

Khanna, B.S., *Panchayati Raj in India : Rural Self Government*, New Delhi, Deep and Deep Publications, 1996.

Kunhaman M, *Development of Tribal Economy,* New Delhi: Classical Publishing Company, 1989.

Mann, R.S. (ed.), *Tribes of India-Ongoing Challenges*, New Delhi, M.D. Publications Pvt. Ltd., 1996.

Mathur, PRG, *Tribal Situation in Kerala*, Trivandrum : Kerala Historical Soceity, 1977.

Mehta, Prakash Chandra (ed.), *Ethnographic Atlas of Indian Tribes*, New Delhi, Discovery Publishing House, 2004.

Mehta Prakash Chandra, *Tribal Development in the Twentieth Century*, Udaipur, Shiva Publishers, 2000.

M.H. Gavit and Attar Chand, *Nehru : Tribal and Women Welfare*, New Delhi, H.K. Publishers & Distributors, 1989.

Mishra, Madhu Sanitha, *Press and Political Socialization*, Delhi : Dominant Publishers and Distributors, 2003.

M. Mohanty, "On the Concept of Empowerment" in Debal K. Singha Roy (ed.), *Social Development and Empowerment of Marginalized Groups : Perspectives and Strategies*, New Delhi, Sage Publications, 2001.

Mukhopadhyay, Amal Kumar, *Political Sociology : An Introductory Analysis*, New Delhi, Bhageweas and Co., 1980.

Narayan, Iqbal, *The Idea, the Image and the Reality in Panchayati Raj*, Delhi, Indian Institute of Public Administration, 1981.

Pandey, A.K., *Tribal Society in India*, New Delhi, Manak Publications, 1997.

Panur, K., *Ente Hrudayathile Adivasi* (Mal.), Kottayam, Current Books, 2005.

Pathy, Jaganath, *Tribal Peasantry – Dynamics of Development*, New Delhi, Inter-India Publications, 1987.

Prabhash, J., *Panchayati Raj* (Mal.), Thiruvananthapuram, Kerala State Resource Centre, 1995.

Prakash, P.K., *Anyadheenappedunna Bhoomi – Adivasi Bhoomi Prasnattinte Charithravum Rashtriyavum*, Kozhikode, Pappiyan, 2002.

Pylee, M.V., *Indian Constitution*, New Delhi, Mittal Publication, 1995.

Raj, Dileep (ed.), *Thantedangal : Kerala Samooha Bhoopatam Muthanga Samarathinu Sesham* (Mal.), Kottayam, D.C. Books, 2003.

Rajora, Suresh Chandra, *Social Structure and Tribal Elites*, New Delhi, Himanshu Publications, 1987.

Rath, Govinda Chandra, (ed.), *Tribal Development in India : The Contemporary Debate*, New Delhi, Sage Publications, 2006.

Rush, Michael and Philip Athaff, *An Introduction to Political Sociology*, London, Nelson, 1971.

Singh, K.S., (ed.), *Introduction – Tribal Movements in India*, Vol. I, New Delhi, Manohar, 1982.

Tripathy, S.N. *Tribals in Transition*, New Delhi, Discovery Publishing House, 1999.

Vaid, Naresh Kumar, *Who Cares for Tribal Development*, New Delhi, Mittal Publications, 2004.

Varyar, Achutha. T.V., *Gothra Sathyangal*, Thrissur, Altermedia.

Velappan, K. *Aadivasikalum Aadivasi Bhashakalum* (Mal.) Thiruvananthapuram: Kerala Bhasha Institute, 2006.

(b) Periodicals and Articles

Baburaj, K.K, *Adivasi Struggle: A Feature and Translation*, Madhyamam Weekly (Mal.), December 7, 2001.

Bijoy, C.R., K. Ravi Raman, *Muthanga – The Real Story: Adivasi Movement to Recover Land*, Economic and Political Weekly, Vol. XXXVIII, No. 20, May 17, 2003.

Bijoy, C.R., *Adivasis Betrayed : Adivasi Land Rights in Kerala*, Economic and Political Weekly, Vol. XXXIV, No. 22, May 29, 1999.

Iyer, V.R Krishna, *Atrocities on Adivasis I & II,* The Hindu, June 16, 2003.

Kunhaman, K., *The Tribal Economy of Kerala – An Intra-Regional Analysis,* Economic and Political Weekly, Vol. XXX, No. 11, March 16, 1985.

Mathrubhoomi Tozhil Vartha : Harisree (Mal.), Kozhikodu, Mathrubhoomi Publication, January 28, 2006.

Nambiar, Malini., *Making the Grama Sabha Work*, Economic and Political Weekly, August 18, 2001.

Prakash, P.K., *Muthanga Vaarshikathil Uyarunna Chodyangal* (Mal.), Madhyamam Weekly, February 27, 2004.

Radhakrishnan, M.G, *Tribal Cleft,* India Today, March 10, 2003.

R, Rajeevan, *Unveiling Injustice Towards Tribals : Kerala Scenario*, Indian Journal of Human Rights and Social Justice, Vol. I, No. 1-2, 2006.

(c) Newspapers

Malayala Manorama

Mathrubhoomi

The Hindu

The New Indian Express.

Index

U